Policing
Henley-on-Thames

From parish constables to the formation
of the Oxfordshire Constabulary in 1857

Andrew William King

Grosvenor House
Publishing Limited

The right of Andrew William King to be identified as the author of this
work has been asserted in accordance with Section 78
of the Copyright, Designs and Patents Act 1988

This book is published by
Grosvenor House Publishing Ltd
Link House
140 The Broadway, Tolworth, Surrey, KT6 7HT.
www.grosvenorhousepublishing.co.uk

A CIP record for this book
is available from the British Library

ISBN 978-1-80381-463-6

Researched & written by
Andrew W. King

(theparishconstable@outlook.com)

Front Cover: Last Church parade of Oxfordshire
Constabulary at Henley-on-Thames, October 1967.

Back cover: End of a Night Watch after Eugene LAMI.
From *A People's Conscience* by S. Gordon & T.G.B. Cocks.
Constable & Co Ltd 1952.

Dedicated to my father
William Alfred King – 1921–2021
Ex-Special Constable 68
Oxfordshire Constabulary

A Constable is a citizen locally
appointed but having authority
under the Crown for the
preservation of life, protection
of property, the maintenance of
order, the prevention and
detection of crime, and the
prosecution of offenders
against the peace[1].

---

[1] Training School book of definitions in the 1970s

Foreword

We have had almost 200 years of 'modern policing' since the foundation of the Metropolitan Police in 1829. This book tells an important story of modern policing that many histories – focused on London and the major cities – have tended to miss. The early nineteenth century saw a growth of local civic governance across the country.

Andrew King's story of the development of modern policing in Henley shines a light on local policing at just that key point: the transition from the pre-modern constable to the beginnings of local police forces. Henley Town council were early adopters, even before the Municipal Borough and County Police legislation of the later 1830s and early 1840s. The book is full of the day-to-day colour of policing in a small town at the beginning of the Victorian era. Henley's own police force lasted more than two decades before being absorbed into Oxfordshire, which, in turn, lasted more than 100 years before becoming part of Thames Valley Police.

However, the twenty-first century debates about the importance of 'neighbourhood policing' – local policing centred on places like Henley – remind us that the 'local' will always be central to good policing. Andrew King has done a great service in his research and has written a really entertaining story of Henley's local policing at a time of great change.

Dr Peter Neyroud CBE QPM CCMI
Chief Constable Thames Valley Police 2002–2006
Associate Professor in Evidence-based Policing and Director of the Police Executive Programme, Institute of Criminology, University of Cambridge.

Introduction

On 28 December 1838 a newly elected parish constable in Oxfordshire, during the early days of the reign of Queen Victoria, was sworn in as follows:

> *I shall well and truly serve our Sovereign Lady Queen and the Bailiffs, her Majesty's Justices of the Peace for this parish in the place or Office of Constable for one year, ensuing or until I shall be duly discharged. I shall see the Peace duly preserved and kept, Hue and Cry pursued according to the Statute, and do all other things relating to my Office to the best of my skill and knowledge. So help me God.*[2]

All parish constables appointed in Henley-on-Thames during this period would have sworn a similar oath. The duties of the parish constables, also known as petty constables, were many and onerous and, more importantly, they were unpaid, except for certain fees and expenses incurred in that role for the apprehension and conviction of an offender.

The author Daniel Defoe, writing in 1714, had spoken of 'the imposition of the office of constable as an unsupportable hardship; it takes up so much of a man's time that his own affairs are frequently totally neglected, too often to his ruin'. Defoe paid £10 in 1721 'to be excused from serving parish offices' in Stoke Newington, London.

---

[2] *Oxfordshire Constabulary 1857–1957 Centenary.* Chief Constable Oxfordshire Constabulary.

To make matters worse, the prosecution of an offender often required the cost to be borne by the prosecutor (normally the victim), which, although it had the potential to deter those victims of crime, also discouraged constables from investigating alleged offences unless they were sure of being reimbursed their expenses – and, even then, only if the resulting court case achieved a conviction. The parish constable's authority extended only as far as their own parish boundaries and there was no requirement for them to cooperate with neighbouring parish constables.

The parish constable would hold the position for a year, often entering into the duties unwillingly, knowing little of what was required of him, for little or no remuneration. He had local connections and was said to be motivated by personal apprehension and to dread making himself obnoxious. His private occupations engrossed his time and, in some cases, he was loath to exert himself in public office and often kept out of the way when called upon for his services for fear of upsetting his peers.

The small parish of Henley-on-Thames has had a constable since at least the thirteenth century; however, the duties of the constable then would not be recognised by today's police officer, or even those constables who served in the nineteenth century.

Henley-on-Thames had no organised or formal police force that we would recognise before the formation of the county force, although attempts were made in 1830 to regularise the police. Two town constables were appointed annually by the mayor (who was also a justice of the peace) and they reported to the town's magistrates. The mayor was responsible for paying the expenses of the constables from the local rates until 1830, when it was decided that for a more efficient police in the town, two constables should receive an annual salary of £10 in order to attracted fit and able men to the role. From this date, salaried constables served for more than the 12 months of the previous parish constables. The constables reported to the mayor and justices of the peace in the town.

The paving commissioners appointed two watchmen under the Bridge Act[3] which allowed for lighting and watching in the town and for regulating the footways and removing nuisances, obstructions and annoyances. The Corporation also occasionally employed beadles.

Henley did not have a watch committee or a borough police force like other neighbouring towns, such as Reading or Windsor. There was no chief or head constable of the town. In most cases, police work would have been ancillary to their main occupations, which they continued during their period of service. The town lock-up was situated in the Guildhall, which occupied Middle Row, in what is now the Market Place, until the late eighteenth century.

In some northern districts of Oxfordshire, police officers were employed by way of voluntary arrangements of the inhabitants – i.e. officers were paid directly by local parishioners to police their area. There is no evidence of this voluntary system being used in Henley. There was, however, a private organisation called the Henley Association for the Protection of Property, which was formed in 1788 and continued for well over 100 years; this is explored later in the book.

As a relatively small parish and incorporated town, Henley-on-Thames escaped the attention that encompassed other larger towns when it came to police reform – especially the Municipal Corporations Act 1835 (5 & 6 Will. IV, c. 76), which required incorporated boroughs to establish a police force under a watch committee composed of members of the

---

[3] The Bridge Act of 1781 established a body of Commissioners enabling tolls to be raised on the bridge as well as setting up the Paving Commissioners.

borough council. In 1851 the Oxfordshire quarter sessions agreed to adopt the Superintending Constables Act 1850 (13 Vic., c. 20), and appointed superintending constables in each of the county's 10 petty sessional divisions. The first superintending constable appointed for the Henley petty sessional division took up his post in March 1851, and the office remained until it was abolished following the formation of the Oxfordshire Constabulary. The superintending constable in charge of the Henley petty sessions division was to become one of only four of the 10 serving superintending constables in 1857 to be chosen to serve with the Oxfordshire Constabulary on its formation. The other three served as inspectors.

The superintending constable had no direct control over the parish constables and was not responsible for their appointment. This led to many superintending constables giving scathing reports about their own parish constables, and their ability to carry out their duties. Some parish constables were unable to read and write and there were instances where the parish constable could not even read the warrant given to him by the local justice. It was examples like this that put the office of parish constable in poor repute throughout history.

Two main events occurred in Henley-on-Thames in 1857, which brought changes to the lives of its inhabitants. The first was the formation of the Oxfordshire Constabulary on 25 March, and the second was the opening of the Great Western Railway station on 1 June. The newly formed Constabulary was perhaps greeted with less enthusiasm than the arrival of 'Virgo', a 'Leo' class 2-4-0T steam locomotive used on the first public train at Henley, which brought its residents and visitors into the age of steam travel.[4]

---

[4] *The Henley on Thames Branch.* Paul Karau. Wild Swan Publications 1982.

The 1857 Oxfordshire quarter sessions had no choice but to accept the establishment of a countywide police force following the enactment of the County and Borough Police Act 1856 (19 & 20 Vict. C69), creating the Oxfordshire Constabulary and sweeping away parochial responsibility for policing in Henley-on-Thames. Henley, however, hung on to their own town constables, as they were entitled to do under the Parish Constables Act 1842 (5 & 6 Vict. cap. 109).

No examples of helmet plates or tunic buttons depicting the town's coat of arms have been identified for the constables of Henley-on-Thames of any period. The style of uniform (if there was any) is also unknown.[5,6] No tipstaff or truncheon has been found that links to the town or its constables. The only hint of a uniform is in a letter of complaint against the police in a local newspaper in 1834, which describes a 'red-collared head-officer'; however, this may have been facetious remark when criticising the police.

The 'Police and Constabulary List' published in October 1844 gives a detailed record of those county, district constabulary forces and local and provincial police forces in existence at that time in the UK. Banbury was the only town in Oxfordshire included in the list, having an organised police force established in 1836, and headed by a superintendent.[7] Henley-on-Thames does not appear on this list.

There has never been a publication dealing solely with the town's police before the County Constabulary was formed. Although records are not exhaustive, particularly in relation to the identity of the parish constables, the frequency of court and police reports in newspapers in the eighteenth and nineteenth centuries, together with quarter session

---

[5] *Badges of Office.* M.B. Taylor & V.L. Wilkinson 1995.
[6] *Police Buttons.* Howard Ripley 1983.
[7] With thanks to the Police History Society.

records, now held in the Oxfordshire History Centre, as well as parochial records, opens a window on some of those men who took on the responsibility of policing the town and the roles they played in keeping the peace.

Here we look at the lives of those men (for it was only men in those days) who lived, worked and policed the town, together with their families, and others who came into contact with them during the course of their duties, including justices of the peace, felons, witnesses, residents and victims of crime. Often details of crimes are reported in local newspapers in detail, but fail to name the constables who investigated the case. Some of these cases have been included chronologically because residents of the town and business owners are mentioned.

Chapter One

Frankpledge

In thirteenth century England, the role of law enforcement was placed on the whole of the community, who were made accountable through the system of frankpledge, whose origin predates the Conquest. Frankpledge was already widespread across southern England. A tything was a Saxon tradition of collective responsibility in which families were grouped in tens – the counties of England were divided into hundreds, and those hundreds into tythings or towns.

Laws passed in the tenth century in the reign of Edgar stated, 'If there be present need, let it be known to the hundred men and let him make it known to the tything-man and let all go forth to where God may direct them to go. Let them do justice on the thief, as it was formerly the enactment of Edmund.' King Canute ordered that enrolment into a tything was compulsory. These arrangements were taken over by the Normans, modified and systematised under the description 'frankpledge'.[8]

The ancient custom was that no man was suffered to abide in England above 40 days unless he was enrolled in some tything. With the advent of Norman rule, each village and township became a feudal manor, or part of a manor. Neither the Normans nor the Danish kings interfered with the English practice of preserving the peace by the method of mutual responsibility and open trial in the hundred courts.

The tything, headed by the chief-pledge or head tything-man, or head-borough, was responsible for apprehending any man

---

[8] *A History of Police in England and Wales.* T.A. Critchley 1967.

of that tithing who was suspected of breaking the law. All men over the age of 12 years who were free and servile were required to be members of the tything and swear an oath of loyalty. The tything was responsible for detaining and keeping in custody any offender until they could be tried at the manor court.

J.S. Burn in his book *A History of Henley-on-Thames* mentions the books and rolls of the court baron (manor court) and view of frankpledge that extend back to the time of Edward III. It is fortunate that one of the rolls of 1351 contains the names in the 'Ville de Henle' (that's how the town's name is spelled in the roll) whose pledges are matched to the names of their sureties. A sample of those names are included below and gives us an insight into those inhabitants who lived in Henley-on-Thames in the fourteenth century and swore frankpledge.

Ward: *Robti le Hore et Ro. Moreys*

Oath pledged by:	Surety:
Rads Pobam	Will. Tendinge
Henr. le Johes de Stoke	Henr. Hering
Will Sely	Thom. de Ponte
Rob. le Rede	Par de Mareis
Nick. Bareter	Thom. Homfrar
Rob. le Pimenter	David Dyer
Reginald Waldence	Thom. Piscator
Elyas de Ponte	Ric. de Arpenden
Rog. de Cochestr	Ric. Hering
Matheus de la Done	Reg. le Noreys
Galfridus de Leuckner	Philipp le Monie
Johes Newman	Thom. Jory
Reginaldus le Buck	Willm. le Berker
Alexander Sanser	Philipp Hanel
Rads. de Clebow	Elyas de Walingford
Johes Sampson	Ric Hain
Nichs. Buke	Reginaldus Pistor
Henr. le Feet	Randulphus de Falley
Adam Stede	Gilbs. de Tirefeld

Rog de Neuhelme
Will. Fulkeley
Johes atte grene
Johes le Gardener
Hugo de Ocle
Johe Toppe
Col. Rikild
King Hering
Biscop Hering
Hugo Pistor

Philipp Stede
Johes Salaman
Adam Cl'icus
Alanus Peleter
Walt's Stanpun
Rads de Assenden
Andr. Padeler
Johes Clabhow
Nich. Aubin
Will. Shadewell

Ward: *Symon Aste & Ade' Clici.*

Oath pledged by:

Surety:

Johes Frauncis
Simon Atte Hill
Robs. Simon
Joh's de Hamelden
Wills. le Rede
Joh'es le Deier

Will's Faber
Johes Finch
Adam le Coter
Rogs. le Deyer
Walts. de Sadeler

Ward: *Willi de Porter & Ric le Chepman*

Oath pledged by:

Surety:

Jeodanus le Sumet'
Reginaldus Brian
Joh'es Wykeman
Thom. Twigge
Jo'hes (Mohu)?
Thom' Wydefule
Joh'e Aubin
Walts. Gauteran
Will' le Glover
Ric. Noel de Hamelden
Henr. Molendin
Hugo de Lenlam

Ric' le Rober
Gilb' le Glover
Jordanus Tilling
Will' le Tyler
? Goldonoy
Joh'es le Luter
Tho' Suter
Joh'es Sadwell
Will' le Grover
Ric. Ate Merse
Will. de Grover
Marchs. Ate Leye

Henley's first recorded peacekeepers

3

The constable & peacekeeping hierarchy

The police constable is the lineal descendant of the medieval 'petty constable', who is first heard of under that name in the year 1252. Petty constable was a parish office. It was an annual role and it was obligatory and unpaid. Since it was obligatory, it often came to be discharged by 'an inferior class of paid deputies'.B. Ifor Evans sums up the role of the petty constable as follows:

> *The constables are the eyes and hands of the Justices of the Peace, the eyes to see by detecting and informing of offences, the hands to act by the service of the Justices' summonses and the execution of their warrants for arrest. But a system which provided the Justices with eyes and hands so ill selected, ill paid, ill organised and undisciplined seems never to have afforded much ground for national complacency.*[9]

The word 'constable' in the thirteenth century covered a number of roles, including high constables of the hundreds and the petty constables of the manor, tythings or vills. The petty or, more commonly, parish constable was appointed from within his community to carry out his duties, normally for one year. He would have made regular presentments (reports) to the local court leet regarding felons, nuisances etc.

The organisation of peacekeeping in cities, towns, counties and boroughs has always been the task of local, rather than central, government. In 1275, Edward I's Statute of Westminster required that 'All men shall be ready to pursue felons'. This was the 'hue and cry' that each man was required to undertake to follow felons from parish to parish until they were apprehended.

---

[9] *Longman's British Life and Thought.* British Council 1941.

Edward I's Statute of Winchester of 1285 went further:

Watching and keeping the peace in cities, boroughs and towns. And the King commandeth, that from henceforth all towns be kept as it hath been used in times past. That is from the day of the Ascension unto the day of St Michael, in every city six men shall keep at every gate, in every borough twelve men, in every town six or four according to the number of inhabitants of the town, and shall watch the town continually all night, from the sun setting to the sun rising. If any stranger do pass them, he shall be arrested until morning and if no suspicion be found, he shall go quit and if they find cause of suspicion, they shall forthwith deliver him to the Sheriff, and the Sheriff may receive him without damage and shall keep him safely, until he be delivered in due manner.

The office of justice of the peace originated from the knights commissioned by Richard I in 1159 to keep the peace. They received full legal status in 1361 (34 Edw. III, cap. 1). Justices were often lords of the manor and they or their stewards presided over the court leet, where petty/parish constables brought their presentments.

The sheriff, previously known as the high reeve and later the shire-reeve, was bailiff of the shire acting on behalf of the king, appointed annually (when the shrievalty of the shire was not an inherited office). The sheriff was responsible together with the lord of the manor for the peace of the whole county. He would also take custody of felons and ensure frankpledge was properly organised. The sheriff also toured the county supervising the shire and hundred courts on a regular basis.

The high constable would have been responsible for the peace in each hundred (Henley-on-Thames being a parish in the Hundred of Binfield), and for being the go-between for the courts and parish constables. He would also have had to attend the assizes to make presentments as well as executing warrants.

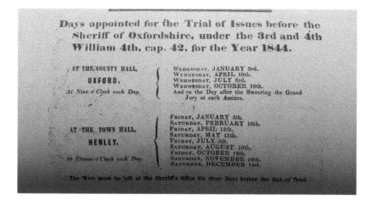

Sheriff of Oxfordshire Court Calendar 1844.[10]

The petty or parish constable for each parish was appointed annually by either the justices or the parish vestry; constables were appointed to keep the peace, arrest felons and convey them to gaol. They were also responsible for supervising watchmen, who were appointed to supplement or supplant the parish constable. Watchmen would have been employed by the parish to take charge during the night. Their duties could include calling out the hours and giving a summary of the weather forecast and generally watching for felons or strangers.

Status

The role of parish constable has often been the subject of derision, particularly in Shakespeare's plays *Much Ado about Nothing* and *Measure for Measure*. Dogberry is portrayed as the bumbling police watchman and Elbow the simple constable, both the subject of ridicule and mockery. We should not view all parish constables in this light. Although many were illiterate and of low status, there were

---

[10] The Book of Henley-on-Thames. GHJ Tomalin. Barracuda Books Ltd 1975.

many who carried out their duties with courage, dedication and fortitude and made their own towns, boroughs and cities a safer place.

In defence of the parish constable, we only have to look at Oliver Cromwell, who explained to a parliamentary committee how he understood his office of lord protector:

> *So far as I can, I am ready to serve you not as a King, but as a Constable, for truly I have, as before God, often thought that I could not tell what my business was, nor what I was in the place I stood in, save comparing myself to a good Constable set to keep the peace of the parish.*[11]

It is very unlikely that Cromwell would have seen himself in the same light as Shakespeare's Dogberry or Elbow, and his speech gives a good impression of parish constables of the seventeenth century and the duties they carried out.

---

[11] The Writing and Speeches of Oliver Cromwell. W.C. Abbott 1937–47.

Chapter Two

Henley-on-Thames parish constables

Very few records exist detailing the names of the parish constables or watchmen who were selected by the Henley-on-Thames vestry to take on this annual task. However, some names have been preserved of those who are known to have served in the town, and the next few chapters will tell what we know of their stories.

In 1542 John **GRAVETT** and Richard **COLLINS** are the first names to be recorded as constables in Henley-on-Thames. They formally received monies that had been collected from taxes on behalf of King Henry VIII.[12]

In 1642 during the civil war, gentlemen and freeholders in the county agreed to pay for the provision of six regiments of horse, amounting to £1,176 per week. This sum was collected by the petty constable (un-named) and paid to the general receiver responsible for this collection. Although the name of the petty constable is unknown, the payment by the town of Henley was £15. In the constable's account book for 1645 are charges for repairing the bridge, 'broken down by military forces, during the Civil War'.[13]

Augustine **SPRINGALL**, between 1592 and 1622, was constable for a period of three years, bailiff for two, bridgeman for five and warden for two years. It was not

---

[12] A *History of Henley.* J.S. Burn 1861. Page 37.
[13] Ibid page 297.

unusual for office holders to hold these positions in succession, first being constables before becoming bailiffs, bridgemen and sometimes wardens in the following years. The office of warden of Henley-on-Thames later became that of mayor.

In 1704 Elizabeth Franwell, widow of Henley-on-Thames, was the plaintiff in a case at the court of chancery. In her bill of complaint, Franwell alleged that Thomas **HARRIS** and William **FOSTER**, both constables of the town, and John Lee, clerk, and John and Christopher Stevens (all being co-defendants in this case) took her into custody on a warrant issued by Jonathan Sayer, justice of the peace and warden of Henley-on-Thames, in June 1703. The constables went to her house and asked her to go to Mr Sayer's house to answer to the charges laid out in the warrant (unfortunately the charges are not specified in the bill of complaint). It was also stated that the constables had seized her violently and carried her out of her house and forced her into the Rose & Crown Inn (Market Place), where they detained her all night and the next day. During this time, Mrs Franwell alleged that the defendants tried to extort money or bonds from her to gain her liberty.

In their defence all five defendants denied the allegations, and stated that while she was in the custody of Harris and Foster, the constables, they had permitted her to be attended to by friends of her choice, and that no demands for money or bonds, notes etc. were made or received by them. Mrs Franwell was released from custody at 4am following her arrest, and when she was taken before the magistrate, Jonathan Sayer, he discharged her because the matter for which she had been arrested had been settled several years before, and because one of the principal witnesses in the case, Daniel Stevens (brother of the two Stevens defendants), was dead. It was apparently the estate of Daniel Stevens that was an issue in this case.

Apparently Franwell had dealt with Daniel Steven's estate, and owed Christopher Stevens £30 from it, but only £20 was paid to him. Franwell had previously lent the sum of £40 to a John Warner, maltster of Henley, and complete settlement of the debt had allegedly not been made, with £10 outstanding, and the argument over who received or did not receive monies was the basis of her arrest. The bill of complaint was brought by Franwell in respect of her 'violent arrest and treatment by the defendants'. Unfortunately there is no record of the outcome of this complaint, but it does give us the names of Harris and Foster, the two constables who policed the town that year.[14] There is a record of Widow Framwell's burial in August 1720 in St Mary's Church burial register.

Another document that survives in the Oxfordshire History Centre is 'An account of the names of Constables and Bailiffs of the town of Henley upon Thames in Oxfordshire, from the year 1715 to this present year 1735'.[15] This document records the names of 40 residents of the town who were constables over a 20-year period in the eighteenth century. The list (shown below) also states that at the completion of their 12 months as constables, each pair then took on the role of bailiff in the town for another year. The year 1721 has no names recorded for the constables

1715. George **HAMPSHIRE** and Sampson **TOOVEY**.

1716. Henry **GREEN** and John **LOVEGROVE**.

1717. John **STEVENS** and Thomas **MASON**.

1718. John **HAVERGILL** and William **DEANE**.

1719. John **BUTLER** and William **WOODHOUSE**.

1720. Thomas **PATEY** and James **LAMBDON**.

1722. George **JEMMAT** and John **SMITH**.

---

[14] National Archives Bill of Complaint C6/410/19
[15] Oxfordshire History Centre. BOR3/C/111/3A.

1723. William **BROOKS** and Abraham **DARBY**.

1724. Stephen **FLETCHER** and William **NEWBERRY**.

1725. John **TOOVEY** and Joseph **DEANE**.

1726. Benjamin **WOOLDBRIDGE** and Thomas **HAVERGILL**.

1727. John **EELES** and John **CASBIRD**.

1728. William **PRAT** and Thomas **JOHNSON**.

1729. Thomas **TAYLOR** Jun. and Henry **ROGERS**.

1730. John **CORDEROY** and Robert **STOPES**.

1731. Samuel **SILLS** and John **HOLLYER**.

1732. Samuel **HUCKS** and Moses **HIGGS**.

1733. William **SHARP** and Peter **STOPES**.

1734. William **BENWELL** and Robert **KITSON**.

1735. Richard **DARBY** and Thomas **SPINDLER**.

In 1751 Mary Blandy was convicted of murder by administering arsenic to her father, Francis Blandy, lawyer of Hart Street, Henley. Blandy was hanged outside Oxford Gaol in April 1752. The story of her trial and subsequent conviction is well known in the town and is not repeated here. Although we do not know the names of the men who would have been sworn as constables during 1751–52, we do know that on Friday 16 August 1751, the mayor and coroner, Richard Miles, issued to the constables his warrant to convey Blandy to the county gaol at Oxford. It was stated that at 4am, very privately and in a Landau carriage and four, Mrs Dean, a servant, and two constables escorted Blandy from Henley to Oxford, arriving at 11am. The warrant reads:

Whereas Mary Blandy of Henley upon Thames aforesaid, spinster, stands charged upon oath before me, with a violent suspicion of poisioning and murdering Francis Blandy, gentleman, her late father, deceased. These are in his Majesty's name to require and command the said constables that you, some or one of you, do forthwith convey the said Mary Blandy to his Majesty's said gaol in and for the said county and deliver her to the keeper thereof. Hereby also requiring you the said Keeper to receive into the said gaol, the body of Mary Blandy, and her there safely to keep until she shall then be from thence discharged by due course of law, and hereof fail not at your perils.

Given under my hand and seal. Richard Miles. Mayor & Coroner.

The two escorting constables would have travelled in style to Oxford in the Landau with Blandy. The more normal mode of transporting prisoners of the 1750s from Henley to Oxford would have been by horse and cart.

During the winter of 1756–57 two Bow Street constables, Robert **STREET** and Robert **SAUNDERS**, sent by the magistrate John Fielding, arrived in Henley in pursuit of William Page, a notorious highwayman who had been active on the Maidenhead to Henley road. Page escaped detection on this occasion; however, he was finally arrested in August 1757, by other Bow Street officers following a pursuit through the home counties.[16] Page was hanged for his crimes in 1758.

In 1786 Robert **LOVEDAY** and John **WHITE,** constables of the liberty of Northfield End, appeared before the court leet in the Manor of Bensington, where they were accused of illegally demanding and receiving money as head-silver[17] from Mrs Sarah Freeman and Mr William Davis of Henley Park. Robert Loveday, constable, was present in court and returned 10 shillings, which was the money he had received.[18] (Northfield End was later transferred from the manor to the Henley petty sessional division, in 1836.[19])

---

[16] *The First English Detectives.* J. Beattie. Oxford University Press 2012.
[17] Head silver or head money was money paid as a tax or capitation fee (Middle English).
[18] *A History of Henley.* J.S. Burn. Page 19.
[19] Statement of Transfer OHC. QS1836/1/A10/3.

Caricature of a nightwatchman with lamp,
rattle and staff. Authors Collection.

Napoleonic wars

The French Revolutionary wars caused consternation throughout the realm, and on 17 December 1792 the mayor, recorder, aldermen, bridgemen and burgesses of the town of Henley-on-Thames unanimously agreed to several resolutions, including:

Taking into their serious consideration of the publick resolution of the Corporation of the City of London, whereby they declare, that it is the duty of all Corporations to preserve their fidelity to the Sovereign, to be watchful for the sacred constitution of the country and to maintain to the utmost of their power, the peace, the property and the personal security of every freeman living under its protection, as it is equally the duty of every freeman to bear true allegiance to the King, and be obedient to the existing laws of the land.

Concerned about seditionists spreading revolutionary ideas in England, the Corporation passed the following resolutions:

That this Corporation regarding as inestimable the blessings which the subjects of the British Empire enjoy under the present government, will use its utmost endeavours to prevent and supress all unlawful and seditious meetings, as likewise the circulation of all mischievous and inflammatory papers within their jurisdiction.

That notice of the above resolution be given to every Publican within this jurisdiction, as likewise that special orders be given to every Constable and Peace Officer, to be particularly attentive to their duty, and give immediate notice to the Magistrates of this Corporation of any unlawful and seditious meeting, and of all persons circulating any papers or handbills, as have a tendency to disturb the publick peace.[20]

The residents of Henley obviously did not feel the need to rise up against the Corporation or the king, for the peace of Henley remained undisturbed.

---

[20] *Oxford Journal*, 22 December 1792.

John ARUNDELL

Arundell is named as watchman, and gave evidence to magistrates who were holding an enquiry into the conduct of several Henley-on-Thames publicans on 7 January 1800. His evidence was about having observed gambling in the White Hart Public House during the early hours of Sunday morning by the landlord, Thomas Burrett, in the company of Thomas Piercey, gentleman. Arundell heard the sound of money being exchanged.

Arundell also deposed that he had heard the sound of gambling on other occasions, when Mr Burrett, Mr Marclues (landlord of the Catherine Wheel), Mr Allnutt (attorney), Mr Appleton (brewer) and Mr Piercey were playing cards on licensed premises during the early hours of the morning.

In later life, John Arundell aged 70 years was the town crier, living with his wife Jane and six other members of his family in Market Place, Henley-on-Thames.[21] There is a baptism record of a John Arendle (sic) in St Mary's Church register, dated 30 December 1770, the son of Robert and Ann. He died in March 1855 aged 85 years.

Richard TAYLOR

Taylor corroborated Arundell's evidence and further stated that he had heard that large sums of money were often played for at Mr Burretts premises.

Gambling on licensed premises was illegal in 1800 (as it is today), although in the above case no further action appears to have been taken by the magistrates.

Whether John Arundell and Richard Taylor were involved in the arrest and detention of 63-year-old Edward Thorn, licensee of the Old White Horse public house, in Northfield End, is not known, but it is possible that they may still have been serving as town watchmen when Thorn poisoned his

---

[21] 1841 census.

servant, 24-year-old Amy Jacobs. Jacobs was five months' pregnant with Thorn's child in March 1800 at the time of her death. Thorn had obtained ratsbane (arsenic trioxide), from a Henley apothecary, which was found in the contents of Jacobs' stomach after her death. Two newspaper articles give the following details of the coroners' court and assize court hearings:

> On 14th and 15th instant, an inquisition was taken by R. Garrard, gent. One of his Majesty's Coroners for Oxfordshire, at Henley upon Thames, on the body of Amey Jacob. The circumstances of the case were as follows:- The deceased was a servant to Edward Thorn, a person occupying a public house in Northfield End near Henley, from her sudden death and the circumstances attending the same, a suspicion arose that she had died by poison. On her body being opened, it appeared, to the satisfaction of the surgeons who performed the operation, that the suspicion was but well founded. Other circumstances concurring it appeared to the jury who took the inquisition, that they would be warranted in giving a verdict to that effect, and that they suspected Thorn, her master (who is upwards of 65 years of age) to have administered the fatal drug. The unfortunate victim of his crime, was far gone with child by him, and this circumstance was supposed to be the ostensible motive for committing the horrid deed. Thorn absconded before the jury reached their verdict, but was taken on Wednesday night, and committed by the Coroner to the county gaol on Thursday.[22]

> At Oxford Assizes, Edward Thorn was convicted of the murder of Amy Jacob his maidservant, by administering poison to her, and was executed last Monday. His deportment, after condemnation, was decent, resigned and penitent and in every respect becoming his unhappy situation. The chain of evidence on this man's trial was perhaps the strongest that ever appeared in a Court of Justice in a case of murder by poison; for it appeared that Thorn had first applied to an Apothecary at Henley

---

[22] *Reading Mercury*, 24 March 1800.

on the subject of the girl's pregnancy, acknowledged that he was the father of the child, and then asked, if there was no way of getting rid of it? And notwithstanding the Apothecary, in the strongest terms, pointed out to him that the consequence of any such attempt must take away the life of the girl, he went to another shop, within a few days, and purchased ratsbane, the deadly poison which was afterwards found in the stomach of the deceased, and had undoubtedly caused her death. This wretched culprit was in the 63rd year of his life.[23]

Thorn was executed on 28 July 1800, in public view, on the drop over the front gateway of Oxford Castle. His body was removed to the Anatomy School and anatomised (dissected).[24] Amy Jacobs had been born around 1775 and was buried on 17 March 1800 in St Mary's Churchyard, Henley-on-Thames. Unfortunately we have no record of the officials who investigated this case.

The Old White Horse Public House in Northfield End.

[23] *Hull Advertiser,* 9 August 1800.
[24] *Reading Mercury,* 4 August 1800.

Edward Thorn had married Mary Ranceford in 1767, at St Mary's Church, Henley, and they had seven children between 1767 and 1773, including twin daughters. Four of their children died as infants. Edward's youngest child Thomas was aged 18 years when his father went to the gallows.

In November 1803 the mayor of Henley, James Cloase, received a circular letter from the home secretary, Charles Philip Yorke, requesting that the town advertise for householders who were not enrolled in the Volunteer Corps, or liable to military service, to engage and come forward and act as special constables.[25] This request was made under the General Defence Act because of the threat of invasion by the French. It was requested that a list of names and their residence be made, and that the special constables would be formed into small divisions, with a superintendent placed at the head of each division by the resident magistrate, who would have the control and direction of the special constables. There is no record of any names of parishioners who volunteered to act as special constables during these troubled times, and fortunately the anticipated invasion never took place.

The English legal system from the late seventeenth to the early eighteenth century had been known as 'the bloody code', due to the large number of crimes for which the death penalty could be imposed. In 1813, there were still over 200 offences that carried the penalty of death in the UK.

A Henley man Robert Sparkes, aged 33 years, was sentenced to death in March 1813 at Oxfordshire Assizes, for the offence of burglariously entering the dwelling house of Jane Grellier, of Henley-on-Thames, in November 1812, and stealing 17 silver spoons and other articles.[26] Sparkes was

---

[25] OHC. BOR3/A/XXIII/5.
[26] *Oxford University & City Herald*, 6 March 1813.

married to Hannah nee Chamberlain, and had eight children, the youngest, Chyrsanna, only 10 months old when her father was sentenced. The records of executions at Oxford Gaol do not show that Sparkes was executed, and it is quite possible that his death sentence was commuted to a term of imprisonment. (There is no record of him being transported, either.) There is a burial entry in the St Mary's Church register for a Robert Sparks, dated 7 April 1841, which may be the same individual. His wife Hannah is shown living in Bell Lane, Henley, aged 68 years, two months after the Robert Sparks burial entry, on the 1841 census.

Private protection

The wealthier inhabitants of Henley-on-Thames and surrounding villages did not solely rely on the endeavours of the parish constable when their property was stolen. In 1788 the Henley Association for Protection of Property was inaugurated. The Association was open to businessmen, property- and landowners etc. to join on payment of an annual fee. Any member who suffered the theft of any property could advertise through the Association for the return of their property on payment of a reward. Part of the reward would be paid by the loser and part by the Association. The following example was reported in the *Police Gazette*:

> *Stolen on the night of Thursday 24th September [1829] or early on the following morning, from a field in the Marlow Road near Henley, a grizzle-coloured gelding donkey, answers to the name of 'Sam', the property of Mr. John Strange, of Henley. Whoever will give such information as may lead to the conviction of the offender or offenders, shall, on such conviction receive one Guinea from Mr. Strange, and the further sum of one Guinea from the Henley Association for the protection of Property. S. Cooper, Secretary to the said Association.*[27]

---

[27] *Police Gazette*; or *Hue & Cry*, 3 October 1829.

Two weeks later, another advert appeared in the *Police Gazette*:

> *Stolen on Sunday morning, the 11th instant, from 'Upper Field', between Upper and Middle Assenden, Oxon, a Store Wether Sheep,*[28] *the property of Thomas Stonor, Esq. Whoever will give such information as may lead to the conviction of the offender or offenders, shall, on conviction receive the sum of Twenty Guineas from Thomas Stonor Esq; and the further sum of Ten Guineas from the Henley Association.*
>
> *S. Cooper, Secretary to the Association for the Protection of Property.*[29]

A notice that appeared in the *Berkshire Chronicle* dated 14 February 1829, advertising a meeting to settle the treasurer's accounts at the Red Lion Inn, lists the names of all those who were members of the Henley Association for the Protection of Property:

List of Members. February 1829.

Mr. Edward A'Bear
Mrs. Alleway
Mr. Joseph Appleton
Mr. Joseph Appleton, Jun.
Mr. Beard
Mr. Robert Belcher
Messrs. Benwell, & Co.
Rev. Thomas Leigh Bennett
Joseph Benwell Esq.
Mr. William Browne Esq.
Mr. Bromley
Mr. Brakspear
Mr. Isaac Butler
Mr. John C. Byles

Mr. Charles House
Mr. Henry Jackson
Mr. William Lamb
Mr. E.F. Maitland
Mr. Joseph Maynard
Mr. Mercer
Mrs. Newell
Richard Ovey
Mr. William Parker
Joseph Phillimore
Mr. Robert Piggott
Mr. John Plumbe
Mr. Richard Potter
Rev. Robert Pritchard

---

[28] A wether is a male sheep castrated before maturity.
[29] *Police Gazette*; or *Hue & Cry*, 14 October 1829.

Mr. Henry Byles
Thos. Darby Coventry, Esq.
Mr. John Chipp
Mr. John Chase
Mr. Thomas Cooper
Mr. Samuel Cooper
Mr. Thomas Crouch
Messrs. Curtis & Tubbs
Mr. Thomas Deane
Mrs. Dixon
Mr. Charles Elsee
Hon. and Rev. Daniel Finch
Mr. Frizer
H.P.W. Freeman, Esq.
Charles Green, Esq.
Rev. A.B. Howman
George Grote, Esq.
Mr. Robert House
Mr. Thomas House.

Mr. John Reeves
Mr. James Reeves
Rev. I.R. Roberts
Rev. Dr. Scobell
Mr. Edward Samey
Mr. James Sharp
Mr. William Soundy
Mr. Sandy
Mr. George Shelton
Mr. John Strange
Thomas Stonor, Esq.
Thomas Toovey, Esq.
Mr. W. Vanderstegen
Mr. Robert Webb
W. Wright, Esq.
Mrs. Atkyns Wright
Mr. Wrigglesworth
Mr. William Young

The Association met regularly for over 100 years, each meeting being held in a local inn and followed by a dinner. The names of the members above include many town officials, including past and present mayors, aldermen, solicitors, business men and women and land owners. From the newspaper reports of the meetings, one gains the impression that the Association over the years became more of a social and dining club for its members.

It was not only the Henley parish constables who took action when crimes were committed, as a newspaper article reports in October 1818:

Thursday last about half past six o'clock in the evening, Mr Pratt, a baker, of Reading, was robbed two miles from Henley, on the road to that place, of a Bank of England £1 note 16s., and a metal watch, by three men, George, John, and Thomas Irby, brothers, residing near

*the Bell and Bottle, between Maidenhead and Reading.
Mr Chinnock, jun., horse dealer of the latter place,
overtook Mr Pratt at the Plough at Shiplake; having been
informed of the robbery, he immediately rode towards
Henley in pursuit of the villains, where he learned
they had passed through on their way to Marlow
fair. Mr Chinnock with Mr Venables, of the Bell Inn,
Mr John Marklew, Jun., [sic], of the Catherine Wheel
Inn, and several other inhabitants of Henley, pursued
and apprehended them all at the White Horse public
house, Marlow, about one o'clock Friday Morning, bought
them back to Henley, and lodged them in the prison
there. The same day they were committed to Oxford Gaol
by the Hon. Reverend Daniel Finch, to take their trial at
the next Assizes for the County of Oxford. A charge was
also exhibited against them by Mr Sadler, butcher, of
Marlow, for stopping, robbing, and beating him on the
highway, near Bisham about three weeks ago.*[30]

The three Irby brothers were convicted of theft and assault
at Oxfordshire assizes on 3 March 1819, and sentenced to
death by Mr Justice Richardson.[31] The sentences were
commuted to transportation for life. They were incarcerated
on the hulk *Justitia*, at Woolwich, until 30 July 1819, when
they sailed to New South Wales on the ship *Recovery*,
arriving in Sydney on 18 December 1819, with 184 other
convicts, and moved to Parramatta, western Sydney, to
begin their exile. All three brothers remained in Australia
until their deaths, John in 1847 aged 50 years, George in
1862 aged 67 years and Thomas in 1874 aged 75 years.[32]
The arrest of the Irby brothers demonstrates that the 'hue
and cry' system of law enforcement was still operating in the
Henley area in 1818.

---

[30] *Windsor and Eton Express*, 25 October 1818.
[31] *Oxford University and City Herald*, 6 March 1819.
[32] British Convict Transportation Register, State Library of Queensland.

Town beadles

A brief report in the *Windsor and Eton Express* dated 15 December 1821 reported that,

> *The town of Henley on Thames some time back adopted the plan of appointing beadles for the sole purpose of ridding the town of beggars. The advantages are evident the streets were before overrun with beggars.*

Another mention of a beadle is made in 1826 when Stephen Williams aged 22 years, John James and Robert Mason were convicted of breaking into the dwelling house of Edward Sherwood of Sonning and stealing copper worth 20 shillings. The three defendants attempted to sell the copper at the shop of Mr May in Henley, informing him that they had purchased it in Reading. Mr May suspected that they had not come by the copper honestly and refused to buy it.

They then sold it to a man in the town for £1 and were taken into custody by the town beadle and constable, who had been watching them. At the Oxfordshire assizes in July 1826, the three prisoners put in a written defence stating they were occasional dealers in metal and they had bought the copper off a person they did not know. They were found guilty and sentenced to death. The name of the beadle or constable who made the arrest is not recorded.[33]

Williams, James and Mason were spared the noose and had their sentences commuted to transportation for life and in August 1826 were removed from Oxford Gaol to the hulks in Portsmouth.[34] James and Mason left Portsmouth on board the ship *Marquis of Hastings* on 14 April 1827 together with 166 other convicts and arrived in New South

---

[33] *Oxford Journal*, 8 July 1826
[34] *Oxford Journal*, 26 August 1826

Wales on 31 July 1827.[35] There is no record of Stephen Williams being transported.

In December 1835, eight years after they were transported, the Reverend James Hitchin, vicar of Wargrave, petitioned for clemency for Robert Mason, on the grounds of his good character and good conduct in New South Wales. The petition was supported by certificates from four officials in New South Wales, including the prisoner's master, testifying to his good behaviour.[36] There is no record of whether the petition was successful. The arrest of Williams, James and Mason is the only report found of the town beadle being involved in the apprehension of offenders and indicates that there was cooperation between the town beadles and constables.

In June 1824, Sir Robert Peel, home secretary, wrote a letter to the chief magistrate in Henley-on-Thames (Thomas Cooper was mayor and magistrate at that time) drawing his attention to the 1824 act of parliament relating to the building, repairing and enlarging of gaols and houses of correction, and for acquiring information that the magistrates have in procuring contracts with the county gaol (4 Geo. 4 Cap. 64). Robert Peel emphasised the strict legal requirement placed on the magistrates, reporting annually to the secretary of state, on the town's contract with the county, on the use of Oxford Gaol.[37]

William HORSLEY

William Horsley is mentioned as a Henley constable when he gave evidence to the Berkshire Midsummer Assizes, held at Abingdon in July 1825. He was born in Shiplake and was married to Sarah, and they had six children – five daughters and one son. William Horsley appears as a constable in records for only 1825, which would indicate he was elected parish constable for that year.

---

[35] British Convict Transportation Register. State Library of Queensland.
[36] National Archives HO 17/130/104.
[37] Oxfordshire History Centre BOR3/A/XXI/1.

The defendant James Reeves was charged that, on the evening of 14 March 1825, he broke into the cottage or dwelling house of John Crutchfield at Wargrave, while there was no one in, and stole a cloth coat, a bible, a table cloth and other articles. William Horsley deposed that he was a constable of Henley-on-Thames and that the prosecutor, Mr Crutchfield, had obtained a search warrant that Constable Horsley executed at Reeves' home in Henley. The stolen property was found in the pigsty and taken into Horsley's possession. James Reeves was found guilty by the jury and sentenced to death by the judge Justice Baron Garrow.[38]

Reeves' sentence of death was reprieved, and he was instead transported for life. He left the UK on the ship *Sesostris* on 23 November 1825, together with 150 other convicts, and arrived in New South Wales on 21 March 1826.[39]

It was the responsibility of the aggrieved, in this case Mr Crutchfield, to make his complaint to a local magistrate, who, if he was satisfied with the evidence, would have issued the search warrant that Constable Horsley executed.

A few years later, in 1841–2, William Horsley was a shopkeeper and dealer in groceries and sundries, corn and hops in Market Place, Henley-on-Thames.[40] He died intestate on 2 January 1857 aged 63 years, leaving personal goods and chattels to the value of £800. Sarah died 18 months later in July 1858 aged 67 years.

One Henley resident, falsely accused of theft, nearly became bankrupt defending himself against prosecution. James Walters, victualler and poulterer of the Crown and Thistle public house, 7 Market Place, was accused of stealing eight

---

[38] *The Berkshire Chronicle,* 16 July 1825.
[39] British Convict Transportation Register. State Library of Queensland.
[40] Pigot's Directory 1842/44.

turkeys from an outhouse belonging to William Whistler, of Hurley, on 21 November 1827. It was to take over two years for him to be exonerated. James Walters, confident of clearing his name, on the advice of his attorney, offered a reward of £10 for the discovery of the offenders. Shortly after the reward was advertised, two persons, a Samuel Woodley and William King, confessed that they were responsible for the robbery, and that Walters had nothing to do with it, and that they were sorry for him, knowing that he was innocent. At the 1828 Berkshire Epiphany Sessions, Woodley and King were acquitted, and Walters was put on trial after Mr Whistler, the prosecutor, positively swore that he saw Walters steal the turkeys. Walters was able to produce an alibi for the time the offence was committed, and was acquitted.

This case surprisingly created a lot of interest in the local newspapers, and the *Berkshire Chronicle* printed virtually a whole page on the two court proceedings. King and Woodley were acquitted despite having made written confessions, it turned out, because of Walter's actions in getting them to admit to the crime. Walters had persuaded King, his servant, to admit to the offence to clear his (Walters') own name, and gave King alcohol, food, money and free board to persuade King to make his confession to the attorney, Mr J.P. Nash, which he did. King also implicated Samuel Woodley in the crime. Mr Walters assured both King and Woodley that they would not be sent to gaol, and gave the two men the reward money for their efforts. For some inexplicable reason, Walters and Nash then took the two men in his cart to the home of Lieutenant-General Sir Morris Ximenes KCH, magistrate and Berkshire landowner, at Bear Court, Hare Hatch, Wargrave, where both defendants re-stated their confessions. The magistrates issued a warrant for their detention at Reading Gaol. Walters then took King and Woodley in his cart to Twyford (stopping on the way at various public houses for refreshment). At Twyford they were both arrested by the local constable (un-named) and escorted to Reading Gaol, where they were held on remand. The judge at the quarter sessions was scathing of these actions of Walters and Nash, both for the manner of getting King's and Woodley's written statements and for not taking them directly before a Henley magistrate to hear their 'confessions'.[41]

Having spent upwards of £100 of his own money in defence of the prosecution against him, Walters was determined, if possible, to bring the real culprit to justice, and issued a notice in local newspapers offering a reward for information leading to the arrest of the offender. At the Oxfordshire assizes held in March 1830, Charles Howse, aged 22 years, also known as Charles House, alias Charles Fullock, a Henley man, with another person (un-named) was tried and convicted of an offence of burglary (not related to the theft of turkeys). Having been sentenced to death by the court and (according to the newspaper) knowing that he was to be transported, Howse made a written statement in Oxford Gaol, as follows:

> *The confession of Charles Howse, who states, that about the month of November 1827, I went to Mr Whistler's farm about two or three in the morning, and that I stole eight turkies, his property, along with others who I do not chuse not to mention, and that James Walters, who was tried at the Epiphany Sessions in March 1828, at Reading, was not concerned in the least in the robbery. Mary Anne Page saw the turkies in question in my possession, at her lodging, previous to their being sold in the market at Uxbridge. I sold them, one for 9s. four for 8s. each, and three for 7s. each. Betsy Willis, of Henley, knew that the turkies in question were placed in Mr Cooper's hovel, by myself in the parish of Remenham. C. Howse, signed in the presence of:-*
>
> *J. Ingram, D.D.*
> *James Grant Governor.*
> *Henry Doswell, Chief Turnkey. Oxford Castle. 5 May 1830.*[42]

---

[41] *Berkshire Chronicle*, 19 January 1828.
[42] *Reading Mercury*, 14 June 1830.

It is not known how Howse's confession came about. It is possible that, being from Henley, he knew Walters and was aware that he had been prosecuted and acquitted and was still trying to clear his name. Whether Walters offered any inducement to Howse, we will never know. The *Reading Mercury* and *Reading Chronicle* newspapers clearly supported Walters' efforts to clear his name, and carried notices requesting that a subscription be opened on his behalf, to place him in 'that situation of life, from which he was, without cause, so suddenly cast down' and to enable him to support his wife and five children, who were currently dependent on parish relief. It was asked that donations be made to Messrs. Hickman and Stapledon's, at Henley Post Office, the *Mercury* office at Reading and at Mr Brown's, Windsor. There is no record of any sums of money that were donated for the Walters family.

The National Archives' Quarterly Prison Returns for 1830 record Charles Howse's death sentence being commuted to seven years' imprisonment. There is no record of him ever being transported, however.

Thomas Alexander LIVINGSTONE/LIVINGSTON

Livingstone is recorded as constable of Henley-on-Thames in 1827–28. He was born in Perth, Scotland, about 1791. In October 1813 Livingstone married Sarah Swallow, a widow, by licence at St Mary's Church, Henley-on-Thames. They had one son. Sarah died in October 1820 aged 48 years.

In 1841 Thomas was living in Duke Street, Henley, with his second wife Emma nee Carter, who he married in October 1822; he is recorded as a shoemaker in the census and in the St Mary's Church baptism register when his four children were baptised. In 1850 Livingstone was working as a house porter at the Henley Union Workhouse, with his wife also working there as an assistant.

Constable Livingstone was named in a newspaper article as having been violently assaulted by Thomas Usher in July 1827. Usher was sentenced to six months' imprisonment at the Oxfordshire quarter sessions.[43] This same case is mentioned in the *Oxford University and City Herald* of 14 July 1827; however, in this newspaper Richard Potter (who himself was to become a constable in 1831) is mentioned with others (un-named) who are reported to have also been assaulted by Usher.

On 21 January 1828, a constable of Henley (no name mentioned), presented a bill of £1 15 shillings to the select vestry, for the remainder of his expenses from the county for the conveyance of Thomas Usher and Robert Harris to Oxford for felony. It was ordered that the sum be paid.[44]

Perhaps the sum was owed to Constable Livingstone, as the arresting officer of Usher. Robert Harris had been charged with stealing a quantity of lead from Charles Henry Chapman and Thomas Bowling of Henley-on-Thames, although Livingstone is not mentioned in the newspaper report relating to Harris' case.[45]

Depression took hold of Thomas Livingstone in later life, when he and his wife were living at Rotherfield Peppard. On Wednesday 14 March 1860, Thomas left his bed at 6.30am and was found around 9am the same day by his wife, suspended by his neck from a rafter in their coal house. He was 69 years old. The inquest was held the following day, Thursday 15 March, at Bolts Cross, Rotherfield Peppard. The evidence was heard as follows:

> *Emma Livingstone stated, I am the wife of the deceased who was a shoe maker by trade. He had been troubled with lowness of the mind for at least four years, and*

---

[43] *Berkshire Chronicle*, 21 July 1827.
[44] OHC BOR/C/111/2.
[45] *Oxford University and City Herald*, 17 November 1827.

lately he has very seldom spoken to me. During the last six weeks he has not said a word for days together. The day before his death he went to Henley and returned home about 5 o'clock, after which he had a pipe, but did not smoke it out, and he appeared very nervous troubled in his mind all the evening, resting his head upon his right hand as he sat by the fireside. The next morning when he got up, he did not speak to me whilst dressing. I came downstairs about half past seven o'clock, and after I had got the breakfast ready, went out to find him, but could not meet with him, nor did he answer by name when I called. I then came indoors, and after drinking a cup of coffee, I went out in search of him, and at last found him suspended by a rope from a rafter in our coal-house, quite dead. I directly called to William Hitchcock, a young man who was at work close by, who came and cut my husband down. He was stone cold, and must have been dead some time.

The jury, under the direction of the coroner John Henry Cooke, consulted for a few moments and then returned the verdict that the deceased destroyed himself while labouring under temporary derangement.[46]

After Thomas's death, Emma moved to Wooley Farm, Hambleden, Bucks, where she worked as a nurse for Alfred Keene, a farmer, and his wife Susanna. She died in June 1875 aged 77 years.

Constable WHITE

In 1829, Constable White is named in a case at the Easter Berkshire Sessions held at Newbury, in April. John Lay was charged with uttering counterfeit coin (putting forged coins into circulation) at the Two Brewers, situated at the bottom of Henley Hill. William Gibbs, the landlord of the

---

[46] *Oxford Chronicle and Berks and Bucks Gazette*, 24 March 1860.

Two Brewers, and his son, J. Gibbs, gave evidence of Lay passing a counterfeit half-crown coin for two glasses of gin on 17 March 1829. Lay was later followed to the Swan Public House in the Market Place, Henley, by the son, who challenged him in the tap room.

White, the constable, was called for and attended the public house. Constable White took possession of Lay's bag, and found 10 half-crowns dated 1819, which were described as 'base coin, worthless, and miserably executed'. Lay, in his defence, said he would leave all to the mercy of the court, and was found guilty and sentenced to 12 months' imprisonment with hard labour. This is the only record known relating to Constable White, whose first name is unknown.[47]

On Wednesday 10 June 1829, the first rowing match between Oxford and Cambridge universities took place on the River Thames at Henley. The event drew a large crowd to the town to witness the spectacle. The police were in attendance to keep the peace and watch for known felons. The *Berkshire Chronicle* had this to say about the event:

> *During the festivities at Henley, on Wednesday last, the police was placed under the care of our active officer, Mr Golding, and we are glad to hear that not a single robbery was committed, although many 'tried' characters were amongst the spectators.*[48]

Constable **GOLDING** was in fact a police officer employed by the Borough of Reading. He was an experienced officer and appears in numerous newspaper reports, investigating and giving evidence in criminal cases in the Reading area. It would appear from the above newspaper report that Constable Golding was drafted into the town to supervise Henley's parish constables for the first ever University boat race, which the Oxford crew won easily.

---

[47] *Berkshire Chronicle*, 2 May 1829.
[48] *Berkshire Chronicle*, 13 June 1829.

Swing Riots

In 1830 the protests against agricultural mechanisation known as the 'Swing Riots' were taking place across southern and eastern England. Local landowners and in particular farmers were concerned that they would be a target of the mob. This was as a result of a letter sent from London to Mr Sharp, farmer of Fawley, and signed 'Swing'. The letter threatened the destruction of his property, together with that of Mr Pope and Mr Bullock, also farmers of that parish. Henley magistrates issued a notice, requiring all well-disposed persons to assemble at the town hall, at 3pm precisely on 23 November 1830, to aid and assist the civil powers. This followed an arson attack on one barley stack and one oat stack at Pishill Farm, belonging to Thomas Stonor of Stonor Park. The fires were extinguished by fire appliances from the Royal Exchange and Mr Stonor's own engines.

A 'strange' person was reported to have been seen in the vicinity of the farm asking questions about the number of farms owned by Mr Stonor, and the number of machines used. This person, who was not named, was detained in Henley-on-Thames and examined before two magistrates of the county, Captain Montague and Thomas Toovey. No evidence was brought against the man that justified the magistrates detaining him.

At the town hall on 23 November 1830, upwards of 109 'respectable' inhabitants were sworn in as special constables for town and county by the magistrates.[49] Many others had also been sworn as special constables in Berkshire and Buckinghamshire to better help with patrolling the neighbourhood that bordered the town.

The effect of the threats against Mr Sharp and others was such that he destroyed his own machine. The steam machine

---

[49] *Berkshire Chronicle*, 25 November 1830.

at Fawley Court Farm was also dismantled and would not be used again on the premises.

A professional police

While the recruitment of special constables was under way, the town council appointed a committee on 3 November 1830, to look into the powers proposed by the Corporation for providing a more convenient gaol and establishing a better police for guarding the town of Henley-on-Thames.[50]

The committee comprised William Young, mayor, Robert Belcher, James Dixon and Samuel Cooper, and was to make two recommendations. The first was to look into providing a more convenient gaol in the town. The committee found that although the charter granted to the Corporation permitted a gaol in the town; it was only for a temporary place of confinement. Although it would be beneficial to have a gaol where prisoners were confined before trial at the sessions, the expense would be considerable and the money could only be raised within the limits of the Corporation.

The second recommendation was to enquire into the current state of the police. In this case the committee were of the opinion that the inefficiency of the police arose because no funds for that purpose had ever been placed at the disposal of the magistrates, and that a small expense could rectify this. The committee further decided that the magistrates should be able to pay the two constables appointed by the mayor an annual salary not exceeding £10 each. The committee recommended that the payments be made by the treasurer of the Paving Act to the mayor, in addition to the sum now paid to him for the wages of the watchmen, an annual sum not exceeding £30 – the sum to be appropriated for the purpose of providing fit and able men as a police for the town, under the powers and authorities of the town's

---

50 OHC. BOR/A/XXI/2.

Paving Act. Here, in 1830, we have the start of salaried and, one would have hoped, professional police officers in Henley-on-Thames. We now see salaried constables in Henley from 1831, who served more than the one year of the previous unpaid parish constables.

Having agreed on a more professional police, committee member Samuel Cooper himself became a victim of crime in February 1831, when Edward Mead(s), was charged with stealing a half part of sundry bank notes, the property of Samuel Cooper, gentleman of Henley. Details of this offence are frustratingly scarce, as the *Oxford Journal* newspaper dated 5 March 1831 printed only a brief text from the Oxfordshire Lent Assizes, stating that the sentence was not reported when their reporter left, because the trial occupied more than three hours, but the evidence was of so circuitous and lengthened a nature that the newspaper abstained from entering into it at all. In the event Meads was found guilty and sentenced to seven years' transportation.[51] There is, however, no record that Meads was actually transported.

At the Henley fair held on 22 September 1831, William Fleming, a professor of the black-art, i.e. dark mystical practices was deprived of the pleasure of levying contributions from visitors to the fair, being committed to prison until Friday, when he was discharged. Several other persons were brought before the magistrates and the (un-named) beadles were ordered to see them out of town.[52] Two sisters, Ann and Elizabeth Bird (natives of Bristol) were apprehended at the same fair and indicted with feloniously stealing from John Sable a silver watch valued at 30 shillings. At the October 1831 quarter sessions, both sisters were convicted and sentenced to seven years' transportation. On 2 April 1832, Ann and Elizabeth sailed on the ship *Hydery* and arrived in Van Diemen's Land on 22 August 1832, with 147 other convicts.[53]

---

[51] *Oxford Journal,* 12 March 1831.
[52] *Berkshire Chronicle,* 24 September 1831.
[53] *Reading Mercury,* 24 October 1831.

At the same quarter sessions, George Pearce, a boy aged 11, was convicted of having stolen a smock-frock from Moses Mascall, of Henley. Pearce was sentenced to be imprisoned for one week and to be whipped.[54]

Another public nuisance to affect the town's inhabitants in 1831 was reported in the *London Evening Standard*:

> *On Monday evening [5 December 1831], between five and six o'clock, a trunk, containing wearing apparel, was cut away and stolen from a post-chaise, whilst ascending the hill at Henley-on-Thames. That town, we understand has been lately swarming with numbers of beggars, some of whom remain for weeks together at the different lodging-houses, annoying the inhabitants by soliciting alms.*[55]

Following the end of the Napoleonic wars in 1815, thousands of unemployed soldiers, many suffering injuries, travelled widely throughout the country looking for employment and causing problems by begging and seeking alms. The Vagrancy Act of 1824 was specifically enacted to punish 'idle and disorderly persons and rogues and vagabonds'. This problem was causing a major nuisance and, as we see in a March 1832 newspaper article, the Corporation was trying to address it:

> *Resuscitation – After a lapse of some years, we are gladdened by the revival of those useful branches of the executives, the daily parading street beadles. We have three now engaged in the duty of clearing our town of the immense numbers of beggars and vagabonds. When we state that the latter has been very considerable of late, we hope those who see, 'no occasion for beadles' will be satisfied that they are highly necessary in this town.*[56]

---

[54] *Oxford Journal*, 22 October 1831.
[55] *London Evening Standard*, 12 December 1831.
[56] *Berkshire Chronicle*, 17 March 1832.

Policing was again discussed at a parish meeting held on Friday 13 January 1832 at the vestry meeting room to consider the propriety of establishing a more effective police for the town, but because local taxes were already considered to be heavy, the meeting decided by a majority of at least 20 to one that they were perfectly satisfied with the present management, and there was no occasion to lay additional burdens on the parishioners.[57] It would seem the changes made by the Corporation in 1830 to establish a paid police force were working satisfactorily.

---

[57] *Reading Mercury*, 16 January 1832.

Chapter Three

On 3 December 1833, Peregrine Bingham and David Jardine, commissioners for the Municipal Corporation Commission (who were to recommend the Municipal Corporation Act of 1835), attended Henley Town Hall to enquire into the running of the Corporation. They heard from the town clerk that, among other town officials, there were currently two constables appointed by the mayor; four called the manor constables appointed by the lord of the manor; and two watchmen, appointed by the paving commissioners.[58]

Two letters to the editor of the *Berkshire Chronicle* by a contributor calling himself 'Verax', in April and October 1834, made scathing comments about the efficiency of the town police and the commissioners appointed under the auspices of the local Bridge Act in respect of Lighting and Watching, accusing them of breaking the law by blocking pavements in the course of their trade:

Hart Street, Henley 17 April

Mr Editor,

I regret being obliged to address you once more, but really the fact of a highway robbery proceeding from a beer shop assemblage, and the loss of our town pump by theft, has induced me to ask my fellow townsmen what can be done in furtherance of that desirable object – an efficient police for this parish? I hear, and I think it a fact, that the sinecure of our red-collared head-officer is increased, in matters. The parish has paid much more

---

[58] *Berkshire Chronicle*, 7 December 1833.

lately than the proposed expenses of the change, and certain it is, we are getting worse.

Yours Mr Editor – Verax.[59]

The theft of the town pump was in fact reported in the *Berkshire Chronicle* on 19 April, when it was stated that:

A bucket and sucker was stolen from our highly ornamented town pump on Friday night, we do not say the Charlies were fast asleep when this happened.

The implication is clear that the author was not impressed with the current state of the town's police.

Mr Editor,

Had your last week's correspondent waited a little longer before he wrote, one of the nuisances he so justly complained of would have been done away with. The poor oyster merchant, who stood at the obelisk, is now no more. I just name the subject by the way to cool your friend's ire, before I proceed to hint to the authorities, that they have a 'paving, lighting and watching Act' and that almost every day some half a dozen tradesmen (shall I be beheaded if I say some of the Commissioners acting under that Act occasionally) incur a penalty for placing goods on the pavement and about the doors, – bales, ironmongery, broker's good, and butter tubs are generally to be seen. Would it be for the fair sex if they got home free from grease and torn garments, but much better it would prove, if some instructions (together with the Act) were given to the efficient police. He (or they) should first give every offender notice of the liability to the fine, and afterwards, if the parties continue to offend, proceed against them. There are other perhaps, at some future period refer to.

Yours truly, Mr. Editor. Verax, Hart Street, Henley.[60]

---

[59] *Berkshire Chronicle*, 7 April 1834.
[60] *Berkshire Chronicle*, 25 October 1834.

It would appear that the correspondent 'Verax' was frustrated that the regulations under the local Bridge Act, which included keeping pavements clear of obstructions, were not being enforced by the police or the watchmen, and that some of the offenders were tradesmen who were also responsible for hiring and overseeing the police. As a resident of the town, Verax had no confidence in those appointed as constables, who he publicly castigated.

Yet another article complaining about the town's police was published in the *Windsor and Eton Express* on 26 April 1834:

Henley, April 25.

Our town has for some few weeks past, been pestered with beggars and tramps. We pay a good sum for our police and we think, with due deference to their scarlet collars, we are entitled to better protection from the annoyance of these paupers.

These complaints from residents of the town were perhaps reinforced by the following case, which came before the magistrates in March 1834, on the type of individuals frequenting the streets:

On Friday Jemima Pearse, a nymph of the pave was charged with stealing a silk gown, the property of Mrs Cox. It appeared that Miss Pearse had been acquainted with Miss Simpson, another lady of the same fraternity, living with her grandmother the said Mrs Cox, with whom also Miss Pearse resided a short time. One day the two Misses took their departure to view the beauties of Windsor, and, after they were gone, the gown in question was found to have gone also. This event proved a 'no go' to Mrs Cox, whose wardrobe was not extensive, and the gown not being forthcoming, but Miss Pearse's bonnet being made of silk of a similar colour, the conclusion was that it once formed part of the valuable article stolen. Mrs Cox, a diminutive dame (known as a dealer in animals of the feline race), possessed of a piercing gimlet eye, and a good personification of the hag in Otway's play of the Orphan, stated that she purchased the gown off one Miss May, for two shillings, and that lady had previously bought it off another Miss. These facts were clearly established. Miss Pearse in defence said the silk for the bonnet was given her by a friend, and she had the article made up at Windsor by a milliner. She was remanded to the prison till evening, that the constable might go to Maidenhead, to ascertain the truth of her statement. On her return he went to the prison for Miss Jemima, but she was discovered in a fit of epilepsy, from which she did not recover for two hours. She has continued very ill ever since and is carefully attended by the Parish Surgeon. As soon as Miss P. is sufficiently recovered, she will be brought up for re-examination. We must rejoice that neither the life, nor full liberty of Miss Pearse hangs on the credibility of the witness, Miss Simpson, or her truly virtuous 'granny'.[61]

This humorous newspaper report indicates that the ladies named were well known in the town. The term 'nymph of the pave' is a nineteenth-century phrase for a prostitute, and the article implies that both Miss Pearse and Miss Simpson had gone to Windsor to ply their trade. Unfortunately the outcome of this case was not reported and the constable who went to Maidenhead to make enquiries is also unknown.

Richard POTTER

Records indicate that Richard Potter was a police constable in Henley-on-Thames over a period of four years, between 1831 and 1834, and it is very likely that Potter was one of the first salaried constables following the Corporation's decision in November 1830 to improve the standard of the

---

[61] *Berkshire Chronicle*, 29 March 1834.

police, and to make them more efficient by paying them a salary of £10 a year (the equivalent of £900 in 2021).

Potter, a Henley man, was born on 3 April 1795, the son of John and Mary nee Absolom. His first wife was Hannah, who died in 1834 at the age of 35 years. In 1841 he was living in West Street, Henley-on-Thames, with his second wife Sarah. Richard had five children with Hannah and four with Sarah. He was a sack maker and later a rope maker.

James Roomes, of West Street, was a respected maltster and farmer in Henley, in 1831 with properties in Grays Lane and New Street. On 3 January 1831, James Cato, aged 45, was convicted at the General Quarter Sessions in Oxford of stealing a quantity of wheat, the property of Roomes. Cato, who had recently been convicted of a felony at Aylesbury, was sentenced to seven years' transportation.[62] He was removed from Oxford prison immediately after his trial and taken to the prison hulks at Portsmouth, where he remained until 15 July 1831, when he was transferred to the ship *Surrey*, and sailed to New South Wales, Australia, arriving there on 26 November 1831.[63] No doubt Richard Potter, a near neighbour of James Roomes, would have known him. Although there is no record of who arrested Cato, Potter was a town constable at that time.

In November 1831, Constable Potter is first named in quarter session documents in a case of larceny against the defendants William Bartlett, 26, and Henry Davis, 24, who were both committed for trial for stealing two pairs of worsted stockings from the shop of Mr J.S. Plumbe in the Market Place.[64] Both were described as London gentlemen. On 28 February 1832 at Oxfordshire assizes, Davis was acquitted and Bartlett was found guilty and sentenced to 18 months' imprisonment.

---

[62] *Reading Mercury*, 10 January 1831.
[63] Convict Records. State Library of Queensland.
[64] *Reading Mercury*, 21 November 1831.

Public dissatisfaction with the town's constables was raised again, at a specially convened public meeting held on Tuesday 13 November 1832, at the White Hart Inn, to contest the conviction of several young men charged with letting off fireworks on 5 November. The convictions, it was stated, with one exception, rested on the evidence of the town's two parish constables, who broke down in one of the charges, having positively sworn to the identity of one of the parties charged but who was proved by evidence to have been at home the whole of the evening.

These circumstances caused a general feeling of dissatisfaction in the town, and the meeting of the convicted parties and their friends was convened (by handbills). Mr F. Sawrey chaired the meeting, and a deputation of four tradesmen, Shelton, Partridge, Ellson and Sharp, were appointed to wait on Mayor James Dixon, begging him to consult with his brother magistrates on the subject and annul the convictions, due to the evidence of the constables, and dismiss them from office.[65]

The mayor consulted with his fellow magistrates, Parker, Plumbe, Crouch and Barford, and after 'giving the matter their fullest consideration' they were unanimously of the opinion that, notwithstanding the constables' mistake over one of the defendants, an error which they were partly led into by the improper conduct of the friends of that defendant, the constables very honestly discharged their duty and that the penalties incurred by the parties should not be remitted.[66]

Unfortunately, none of the defendants' or constables' names are mentioned in these newspaper reports. One of the constables who were serving at this time was Richard Potter; the second constable who served with him in 1831 is unknown.

---

[65] *Reading Mercury*, 19 November 1832.
[66] *Reading Mercury*, 26 November 1832.

In December 1832, Potter arrested Thomas Jones for stealing five rabbit skins from Eliza Ovey, of Henley-on-Thames. Jones was sentenced at Oxfordshire quarter sessions to three months' imprisonment and kept to hard labour.

In April 1834, John Douglas was committed to the County Gaol, charged with stealing a quantity of hemp, the property of Richard Potter – in this case, Potter was the aggrieved party and not acting as a constable. Douglas was sentenced to three months' imprisonment in April 1834.[67]

As well as running his other businesses, Potter was the Henley-on-Thames agent for the Sun Life Fire Assurance Society in the 1830s, with his name appearing in newspaper advertisements on many occasions. He was also a member of the Henley Association for the Protection of Property. On 8 March 1843, Potter filed for bankruptcy with debts of just under £300, to the Court of Bankruptcy in London.[68] This did not stop him, however, becoming the licensee of the Kings Arms Public House at 32–34 Market Place, between 1847 and 1877.[69]

Potter did fall foul of the law in 1873 when, as landlord of the Kings Arms, he was prosecuted and fined 1 shilling and 10 shillings costs for selling a quart of ale after 11pm.

Richard Potter retired to Beechwood Cottage, Nettlebed, where he died on 6 December 1879, at the age of 85 years. In his will, his personal estate was valued at under £800. Sarah Potter had predeceased Richard when she died in March 1875 aged 65 years.

---

[67] *Oxford University and City Herald*, 12 April 1834.
[68] *Oxford Journal*, 11 March 1843.
[69] *Hostelries of Henley*. Ann Cottingham 2000.

James LOFTING

Constable James Lofting appears to have had a short career in policing, as records show him to have been active in the role only in 1833. Lofting was also a Henley man baptised in the town in April 1798, the son of William and Ann nee Spratley.

In November 1833 Constable Lofting was named in a recognisance relating to a case against the defendant Ann Cooper. Cooper was charged with stealing a quantity of white rags, the property of James Burnham of Henley-on-Thames, and was sentenced to two months' imprisonment in January 1834.[70]

No further records exist for James Lofting in his role as a constable after 1833. He is found on the 1851 census aged 53 years, single and working as a shoemaker and living with his ex-police colleague, Richard Potter and his family in the Kings Head, Market Place, Henley-on-Thames.

In 1861 James Lofting was living at 11 Church Yard (Alms House), Henley-on-Thames, still working as a shoemaker. He died there in August 1865, aged 69 years. It would seem that James Lofting remained a bachelor throughout his life.

Thomas SMITH

Constable Thomas Smith is mentioned in this interesting notice published in the *Reading Mercury* on 15 December 1834. No other record has been found of Thomas Smith in his role of constable in the town in 1834 or any other year.

---

[70] *Oxford University and City Herald*, 4 January 1834.

WHEREAS I, JOHN RICHARDSON, of Henley-on-Thames, Whitesmith, did, on Monday the 8th of December instant, unlawfully Assault and Ill-treat Mr. THOS. HUNT, Constable of the Parish of Remenham, while in the execution of his duty, for which he justly ordered a prosecution against me, but hath leniently consented to forego the same upon my making a public apology for such my misconduct, and paying all expenses attending the same: I do therefore hereby apologize for the same accordingly, and beg the pardon of him the said Mr. Hunt. Witness my hand, the 10th of December, 1834,

JOHN RICHARDSON.

Witness, Thomas Smith, Constable of Henley.

Thomas Smith mentioned in the *Reading Mercury* notice, 15 December 1834.

John MOSS

It is possible that Constable John Moss also only served for a short period of time in Henley-on-Thames, as records relating to his service are for the year 1834 only. It seems likely that Constable Moss took Lofting's position when he left. John Moss was born in 1803 in Cholsey. In census records he gives his occupation as machinist/engineer and he resided in Northfield End with his wife Elizabeth and seven children.

The first recorded case that confirms Moss's role as a constable in Henley-on-Thames was in January 1834 when the defendant, Walter Owen, together with Richard Sergeant, was convicted by the Henley magistrates of poaching with a net in part of the River Thames rented by the Henley Fishing Society. Both were fined £1 15 shillings. Owen failed to pay and was remanded to the custody of Constable Moss, from which he made his escape. When he was recaptured, Owen violently resisted arrest and assaulted Moss. He was remanded in custody to Oxford Gaol in February and pleaded guilty at the Oxfordshire Lent Assizes and was sentenced to two months' imprisonment in March 1834.[71]

---

[71] *Oxford University and City Herald*, 8 March 1834.

Walter Owen was to commit further offences in 1837 and he pleaded guilty together with John Crane, aged 22 years, a coachman and groom, to the theft of brooms from John Freeman and one case of breaking into and entering the home of John Simmonds Plumbe and stealing silk handkerchiefs and waistcoat pieces. Both were ordered to be transported for seven years.[72] Owen and Crane left the UK on 29 July 1837 on the ship *Susan* and arrived at Van Diemen's Land on 21 November 1837.[73] Owen was convicted of minor offences while in Van Diemen's Land, including being drunk in August 1839. He was also absent without leave in 1840 and had a second offence of being drunk in 1841, when he was sentenced to seven days in solitary confinement. In 1844, having completed his sentence, he was granted a Free Certificate. This certificate of freedom had been introduced because of the need for former convicts to prove that they were in fact free. By the Bushranger Act 1830, anyone could be detained on suspicion of being a runaway convict unless they could produce proof of free status. On completion of their sentences, convicts would make a declaration to the local magistrate, who would check the records. If all was in order a certificate was issued after a fee had been paid. A certificate of freedom was only available to a convict with a finite sentence of seven, 10 or 14 years, because it showed that a sentence had been completed. Convicts with a life sentence could receive a pardon but not a certificate of freedom.

Crane continued to further his criminal career in Van Diemen's Land when, in February 1841, he was sentenced to six days' imprisonment in solitary confinement for attempting to escape and in May 1841 he was sentenced to 10 days' imprisonment for breaking into a public house. In April 1846 Crane was convicted at Hobart court of stealing 11 yards of muslin de Laine, valued at 12 shillings, the

---

[72] *Oxford Chronicle and Reading Gazette*, 4 March 1837.
[73] British Convict Transportation Register. State Library of Queensland.

property of his master William Robertson. Interestingly he was sentenced to be transported for 14 years and to be sent to Port Arthur Penitentiary for four years. Crane was granted a pardon on 25 August 1857.[74]

Perhaps it was the violent assault by Owen that curtailed John Moss's police career in 1834, or could another incident in December that year have been a deciding factor for him to give up his police duties? During the evening of Tuesday 16 December 1834 two men were taken into custody by Windsor police for highway robbery near Henley. The offenders were escorted to Henley from Windsor by a Henley constable. As they proceeded across Maidenhead Thicket towards Henley, the two men, although handcuffed together, made their escape from the gig they were being transported in and were not seen again.[75] The newspaper article does not name the constable or the prisoners and there is no record of them being recaptured and tried at a later date.

John Moss machine maker appeared as the prosecutor, and not as a police officer, in a case at the Oxfordshire quarter sessions in July 1853, when his employee Richard Stevenson was convicted of stealing a half sovereign the previous January. Stevenson was gaoled for one month.[76] John Moss died in October 1878 aged 78 years. His wife Elizabeth died seven years later in March 1885 aged 79 years.

---

[74] Tasmania Libraries online convicts records.
[75] *Windsor Express*, 20 December 1834.
[76] *Oxford University and City Herald*, 2 July 1853.

The Moss Agricultural Machine workforce in Northfield End.
John Moss is pictured in the top hat on the left.

Municipal Corporations Act 1835

Henley in 1835 was not affected by the Municipal
Corporations Act in terms of its policing requirements. As
an ancient borough it was deemed to have an efficient and
popular corporation for the small community. As the mayor
or town magistrates already appointed two constables
annually, the town was spared the requirement to appoint a
watch committee to oversee and appoint police constables
under the Municipal Corporations Act.

Chapter Four

Henry STEPHENS

Henry Stephens became a police constable in 1834 and was to become Henley's longest continuous serving nineteenth-century salaried constable. Quarter sessions and newspaper records and church registers indicate that Constable Stephens served until 1862, continuing as a town or parish constable for five years after the formation of the Oxfordshire Constabulary.

Henry Stephens was born in the parish of St George's, Hanover Square, London in 1806. A carver and gilder by trade, he married Sarah nee Long when she was 16 years old at St Mary's Church, Henley-on-Thames. Sarah was the daughter of George William and Caroline Long.

In 1841 Stephens was living in Gravel Hill, Henley, with his wife and four children. Ten years later, in 1851, he gave his occupation as police officer and was living at 1 Albion Place, West Street, Henley-on-Thames, with Sarah and their seven children and Henry's 76-year-old father.

Stephens is first mentioned in a newspaper report in October 1834, when he carried out surveillance of two women, two men and a child, suspected of uttering counterfeit coin in the town, and is described as 'our active police officer'.[77]

One of his earliest court cases was at the Epiphany Quarter Sessions in January 1835, when Richard Lewington was found guilty of assaulting Stephens in the execution of his

---

[77] *Berkshire Chronicle and Bucks and Windsor Herald*, 25 October 1834.

duty. The circumstances of this assault are detailed in Stephen's written 'Information and Complaint' that he laid before two magistrates, the mayor Mr T.W. Jeston and Thomas Crouch, on 15 November 1834. The magistrates committed Lewington to Oxford Gaol for trial.

Stephens stated:

I am the Police Officer for Henley, on Thursday last between four and five o'clock in the afternoon I was sent for to a house of a person named Lewington in Henley where there was a disturbance. I went there and saw the father of the prisoner bleeding at the nose which he stated had been done by the prisoner, Richard Lewington. I went towards the prisoner and he shortly after struck his mother in my presence and I interfered and the prisoner seized the tongs from the fire place and struck at me which blow I avoided, and closed with him and he struck me several blows and kicked me in the loins, my arms are much bruised and I have been obliged to have medical aid for the injury in my loins. While I was conveying the prisoner to the lock up house, he struggled to get his hands to his side pocket which as I suspected he wanted to get a knife I prevented. I afterwards demanded the knife of him and he took it from the pocket where he had before tried to reach, he appeared quite mad at the time I took him into custody and I have no doubt if he could have got hold of any weapon, he would have done anyone a serious injury. Henry Stephens.[78]

Lewington was sentenced to four months' imprisonment, with 14 days' solitary confinement. He was also ordered to find two sureties of £10 each and his own surety of £20 to keep the peace for one year.[79] Lewington was often in trouble

---

[78] OHC. QS/1835/1/L2/6.
[79] *Oxford University and City Herald*, 10 January 1835.

with the town's police and made several further court appearances for various offences and was regularly reported on in the local newspaper.

Constable Stephens was able to supplement his police wages by claiming a reward following the apprehension of a wanted person. On 15 September 1835, he brought William Harrington, a pauper, before the board of guardians at Henley Workhouse.

Harrington had left his family chargeable to the parish of Pyrton. The board resolved that he be taken before the magistrates to be dealt with according to the law. On 22 September 1835, at the next board meeting, Stephens (who spent four days looking for Harrington) was awarded expenses in apprehending Harrington plus a reward.

Constable **GODFREY** of Watlington was also awarded expenses in endeavouring to apprehend Harrington. There is no mention of the sums paid to either constable. Harrington was sent to prison and, on his release in December 1835, applied to be admitted to the workhouse with his three children. This was granted.[80]

Henry Stephens took his police duties seriously. He was described as a vigilant and efficient police officer, as this article in the *Berkshire Chronicle*, dated 26 September 1835, informs us, only one year after his appointment:

Henley

There is every reason to hope the parties concerned in the late daring highway robberies near our town will be brought to justice through the activity of Stevens [sic] our police officer. William Fisher, alias Curly Will, the leader of the gang, was apprehended on Saturday at Hounslow

---

[80] *Henley-on-Thames Poor Law Union and Workhouse Records.* Oxfordshire Black Sheep Publication 2008.

and will be committed for trial at the next assizes. Our pleasure fair on Wednesday was pretty well attended. Two young men named Gore were apprehended during the day for robbing a public house of a gun and other articles. The men robbed Mr Heath of the White Horse Inn after he had taken them in for several days. They then decamped in the night with every portable item they could lay their hands on. They were taken yesterday by Mr Stevens our vigilant police officer. Our police force has been more than usually efficient during the fair and it may truly be said that the light-fingered flock have never been so well tended before. Several are in custody.

Apart from Constable Stephens, no other constable is named at this time. No record or newspaper report identifies another Henley constable in 1835.

George Jones, alias Samuel Biddle, aged 26 years and a native of Bristol, appeared before Oxfordshire quarter sessions on 26 June 1837, charged with stealing a quantity of lead piping from Mr William Liddesdale of Kintbury, Berks. Jones tried to sell 32lb of lead piping to John Lloyd, shopman at an ironmonger's in Henley-on-Thames. Henry Stephens gave evidence that he took Jones into custody, then searched some fields close to the town and found a sack with about 114lb of lead pipe inside. The pipe found by Stephens matched the pipe sold to Lloyd and corresponded with the remaining pipe in the possession of Mr Liddesdale.

Jones was found guilty of theft and sentenced to seven years' transportation. He was transferred from Oxford Gaol to the hulks at Portsmouth in June 1837, and on 11 April 1838 he sailed from Portsmouth on the *Lord William Bentinck*, with 319 other convicts, and arrived at Hobart on 26 August 1838.[81]

---

[81] British Convict Transportation Register. State Library of Queensland.

In March 1838 Constable Stephens gave evidence at Oxford Lent Assizes against Frederick William Walkling for robbing his employer Mr Plumbe of £300 worth of Irish linen, French and Scotch cambric, silk handkerchiefs and other articles. John Simmons Plumbe owned a draper's shop in Market Place, Henley-on-Thames, and Constable Stephens gave evidence of executing a search warrant and finding the stolen linen in the home of Walkling, hidden under some coals.

Walkling pleaded not guilty but was found guilty by the jury. Judge Baron Gurney, in sentencing, remarked that it was the worst case of this description that he had ever met with, and that he would not be discharging his duty if he did not impose the highest punishment the law allowed: transport for 14 years.[82]

A Mr F.W. Jeston, surgeon, and 49 other Henley residents raised a local petition asking for clemency, because Walkling suffered from fainting fits and was likely to die, which was supported by a medical certificate from Edward Young, surgeon. Despite this, Walkling at the age of 36 years was sent to the prison hulk *York* berthed at Gosport, Hampshire.[83] He was then transported to New South Wales on the ship *Portsea* on 24 July 1838, with 239 other convicts. He arrived in New South Wales on 18 December 1838.[84]

Although the sentence appears severe, Walkling's predicament was probably exacerbated because he stole from his employer John Plumbe, who was also an ex-mayor and magistrate in the town. Also, the sum of £300 in 1838 would be the equivalent of £34,011 in 2021, which may account for the judge's comments on sentencing.

---

[82] *Oxford Chronicle*, 10 March 1838.
[83] National Archives HO 17/66/46.
[84] British Convict Transportation Register. State Library of Queensland.

Prison register showing Walkling's conviction (second entry)[85]

In the same month Stephens also gave evidence in the assize court against William Farmer, aged 19 years, who he had arrested at Henley for uttering two counterfeit shillings on 20 and 21 February 1839. Farmer had passed a one-shilling piece in exchange for goods to Mary Walker and another to Matilda Osborne, both shopkeepers in Henley. On searching Farmer's lodging room, Henry Stephens found another counterfeit shilling. Farmer was found guilty and sentenced to 18 months' imprisonment with hard labour.

---

[85] TNA: Home Office Criminal Registers 1782-1876

Chapter Five

County Police Act 1839 (2 & 3 Vict. C93)

In 1836, the Whig government appointed a royal commission to look into the best means of establishing an efficient constabulary force in the counties of England and Wales (also known as the Chadwick report). Sir Edwin Chadwick, social reformer, argued that there should be a professional police force based on the Metropolitan model. During the course of the County Police Bill there were discussions in parliament and, as a result of opposition from various municipalities, the bill was amended to exempt from this legislation all incorporated boroughs. This allowed boroughs like Henley-on-Thames to opt out of the County Police Act 1839. The act was therefore also known as the Permissive Act.

Only eight counties – Durham, Essex, Gloucestershire, Hampshire, Lancashire, Leicestershire, Wiltshire and Worcestershire – adopted the Act at first and set up police forces in 1839. Within the next two years 16 other counties followed, but this did not include Oxfordshire and 19 other counties were still not included.

The decision for Oxfordshire to opt out was taken by a sitting of the Easter Oxfordshire Quarter Sessions in April 1840, when the magistrates voted 16 for and 33 against the County Police Act.[86] This rejection of the County Police Act in Oxfordshire was greeted with relief in some quarters, by

---

[86] *The Oxford City and County Chronicle*, 11 April 1840.

those who described the act as 'a system of espionage and tyranny utterly at variance with the spirit and practice with the British Constitution'.

The costs associated with setting up a rural police force were also examined by the Oxfordshire magistrates during their deliberations. Buckinghamshire had adopted the Act after 1838 and the annual expense of its force was found to be £3,895 2s 4d, with a further £480 spent on clothing and equipment, which was added to the county's annual taxation.

We don't know Constable Stephens's thoughts on a county constabulary; however, his skills and professionalism were to be tested in a murder in which he was a principal investigator, in May 1839.

Fanny Phillips, a widow aged 84 years, who resided alone in a cottage on Woodcote Common, was attended on by a neighbour Mrs Mary Lambden. Fanny Phillips was put to bed on the night of 7 May 1839 and on her departure Mrs Lambden locked Mrs Phillips in her cottage, as was her usual habit. The following morning, when Mrs Lambden returned to the cottage, she was alarmed to find the door standing open. Without entering she ran to her home and alerted her husband James, who went to the cottage and found Fanny Phillips dead with scratches on her finger where her wedding ring had been forcibly removed. Her body and bed linen were covered in blood and her head was badly bruised.

Adam Duff, the local magistrate who lived nearby in Woodcott House, attended the scene and found a bag containing various tools that did not belong to the deceased. Constable Stephens attended the scene of the murder the same morning, received the bag of tools from Duff and took charge of the investigation. It was quickly established that a local farm worker had recently enquired of his colleagues how the widow supported herself financially and was she not afraid of living alone in her cottage. This labourer was Charles Morley, aged 34.

Richard Lewis, a beer shop keeper, told the police that Morley had attended his shop on five occasions on 8 May to purchase beer, which he paid for with a half-crown piece. Mr Lewis noticed that Morley had other shilling pieces in his purse when he made these purchases.

Mr John Hoare, a sawyer from Goring, identified the tool bag found outside Mrs Phillips' cottage as having been stolen from him while he had been working in College Wood, South Stoke, on 26 March 1839. The bag contained three files, two pairs of compasses, a line and reel, and a saw net. When Constable Stephens showed the bag and tools to Hoare, he identified the items as his, with one file missing.

Constable Stephens searched Mrs Phillips' cottage and found that the front door had been forced open with a bar to gain access. Stephens then arrested Charles Morley for the theft of the tools and searched Morley's own cottage in Newry Green. He found a file hidden in the chimney corner. When the file was shown to Morley, he denied it was his and said he knew nothing about it, although he appeared very agitated. Morley later changed his story and said that he had found the file about five weeks earlier at a handpost (a signpost) on the corner of Deadman's Lane. John Hoare identified the file as the one that had been stolen with his bag of tools. Stephens didn't have enough evidence at this time to charge Morley with murder, so for now the arrest was only for the theft of Hoare's tools.

Adam Duff JP wrote a letter on 12 May 1839 to the home secretary, John Russell, as follows:

My Lord

On the night of Tuesday last the 7th inst., an atrocious murder was committed on the person of an aged woman named Phillips who lived in a cottage by herself, on Woodcote Common, it is but a short distance from my house. Early on Wednesday morning information was brought to me of what had happened, where I proceeded instantly to the spot as speedily as possible. I got a Police Officer from Henley and caused every exertion to be used to discover the perpetrators. As yet I regret to say he has not succeeded.

My object in this addressing your Lordship, is to entrust for your Lordship a consideration the Government offering an additional reward to the sum of £100, which some of my neighbours and self, intend offering to anyone who will give such information as may lead to the discovery and conviction of the party or parties concerned in the murder. As we find difficulty in obtaining any clue, it would greatly assist our efforts if the proclamation of the reward also included an offer of pardon to any accomplice who will give the necessary evidence for the conviction of the murderer.

I have the honour to be my Lord. Adam Duff.[87]

Whether the home secretary agreed to match the reward is not known and no mention is made in any newspaper report.

Morley was committed to the Oxfordshire quarter sessions, where, at his trial on 1 July 1839, he was charged with feloniously stealing on 26 March a quantity of tools valued

---

[87] National Archives HO-64-9.

at 5 shillings, the property of John Hoare. Morley pleaded not guilty but was found guilty and sentenced to seven years' transportation. He had previous convictions for larceny in May 1824 and December 1836, for which he had received six weeks' and six months' imprisonment with hard labour respectively.

On 28 July 1839 Constable Stephens, with William **HAM**, constable of Woodcote, and Henry **GILES**, constable of Nettlebed, returned to Morley's cottage and conducted a further and more thorough search of the property. They removed the thatch from the roof and Stephens found two bags lying on a rafter near the top of the house, about 4 feet from the eaves. One bag contained 232 sovereigns and 10 half sovereigns, and the other held 19 guineas, 10 half guineas, two half sovereigns, a seven-shilling piece and an old silver coin.

Morley remained at Oxford Gaol following his conviction in July 1839 for the theft, until he was transferred to the prison hulks in Woolwich, awaiting transportation. On Friday 24 January 1840, however, Constable Stephens travelled to the hulks at Woolwich and escorted Morley back to Henley. Based on 20 witnesses' evidence, Morley was committed by the magistrates to Oxford Gaol charged with the wilful murder of Fanny Phillips.

Morley's trial began at the Oxfordshire assizes in March 1840. The first witness, Fanny Phillip's niece, Mrs Sarah Kent, stated in her evidence that she identified one of the money bags as belonging to her aunt – she had seen it often. She had seen her with a bag similar to the second one but could not positively identify it as belonging to her aunt. Mrs Kent's daughter Fanny also identified the small bag as belonging to her great aunt. Further evidence identifying both bags as belonging to Fanny Phillips was given by Thomas Kent, her great nephew.

Constable Stephens gave evidence of finding the money in the rafters of Morley's cottage and arresting the defendant at Morley's trial. While he was on remand at Oxford Gaol, Morley had met Joseph Blackall, a fellow inmate who was later acquitted of sheep stealing. Morley had boasted to Blackall that as they were both near neighbours, he (Blackall) would want for nothing, because Morley had more money than any fellow who had come into this house (meaning the gaol). Blackall doubted Morley's assertions, but when Morley asked Blackall if he knew the little house near Mr Duff's, which he said he did, Morley then replied, 'That was where the old woman lived that I murdered.' Morley further stated that when he entered the cottage, the old woman rose up and he hit her three times, which was enough to kill her. He found a 'rare swag of money', which he carried home and put up in the thatch. It was this information that had led Constable Stephens and his colleagues to return to Morley's home and conduct the more thorough search.

Henry Burgess, brother-in-law to Morley, deposed that he had visited him while he was incarcerated on the prison hulks at Woolwich, awaiting transportation on 24 November 1839. During their discussions Morley admitted to Burgess that he had hidden Fanny Phillips' wedding ring in his razor case. As a result of this information, Mr Burgess informed Mr Duff, the magistrate, who went to Morley's mother's cottage where Morley's wife was now living, and he did indeed find a ring stuffed in the bottom of a razor case.

Mary Lambden, recalled as a witness, identified the ring as belonging to Mrs Phillips, by the thickness of the metal and the indentations in it.

Despite an impassioned plea by Mr Rickard, defence barrister, who stated that the evidence amounted only to circumstantial evidence and that Blackall's testimony should be treated with caution, the jury retired for only

10 minutes before announcing their verdict of guilty. The judge, Mr Justice Patteson, placing the black cap on his head, told Morley that he had been found guilty on very clear testimony and nobody who had heard the evidence in court could entertain any doubt of his guilt. He then sentenced him to death. Morley addressed the court, saying, 'I can assure you all, gentlemen, I shall die innocent if I die for this.' He was executed at Oxford Gaol on Monday 23 March 1840. He went to the scaffold protesting his innocence.[88]

This case is interesting because Constable Stephens, although a Henley-on-Thames constable, appears to have taken the lead in the investigation and arrest of Morley, and worked together with other constables from Nettlebed and Woodcote, in a very early example of the Henley petty sessional constables coming together to investigate a murder in one of their parishes.

The new Oxford assize court opened in 1841.

---

[88] *Oxford Journal*, 28 March 1840.

In 1839, the poultry yards on the banks of the River Thames near Henley Bridge were regularly plundered. Henry Stephens suspected Richard Lewington and Joseph Ashley, a proprietor of an Oxford barge, of the thefts. It was frequently remarked that Ashley's barge was often in the vicinity when the thefts took place. Constable Stephens laid a trap, the result of which was that he boarded the barge and found two fowl and five ducks, the property of Mr Swallow, Market Place, Henley-on-Thames. Lewington was charged with stealing and Ashley with receiving stolen property. Both were committed to gaol for trial at the quarter sessions.[89] The outcome of this case is not known, but Lewington was no stranger to trouble. In November 1830 he had found himself placed in the stocks at Henley for six hours, for drunkenness and ill-usage to his parents.[90]

A case of manslaughter at Henley in June 1843 attracted very little attention from the newspapers – only two lines of newsprint in the *Reading Mercury*. On 13 July 1843, at the Oxfordshire assizes, William May, Junior, was sentenced to one week's imprisonment for the manslaughter of James Blackall.[91] No further information has been found regarding the circumstances of this case, though the sentence appears to be very lenient. The 1841 census shows that May, who was living with his parents in West Street, Henley, would have been 22 years old at the time of the offence. Blackall was aged 47 when he died and also lived in West Street, with his wife Jane and four children. His burial took place on 28 June 1843 at St Mary's Church.

In April 1842 the clerk to the Henley Union, Nicholas Mercer, advertised a reward for information on the whereabouts of a George Pratt. Pratt had absconded, leaving his wife and family chargeable to the parish of

---

[89] *Reading Mercury*, 17 August 1839.
[90] *Reading Mercury*, 8 November 1830.
[91] *Reading Mercury*, 15 July 1843.

Henley-on-Thames. It seems, from workhouse records, that George Pratt had left his home in Northfield End on 9 June 1837. He left his wife, Kezia, aged 32 years, and children (Lucy Ann aged nine, George seven, Sarah five, Thomas three and Mary one) to fend for themselves.[92] The below newspaper notice appeared three years after he deserted his family. Presumably as Kezia and the children were still being supported by poor relief, the advertisement where Pratt was suspected to be living was an attempt to find him. There is no evidence that Pratt was ever traced.

TWO GUINEAS REWARD.

WHEREAS GEORGE PRATT, aged about 38, of Henley-on-Thames, in the County of Oxford, lately ABSCONDED, leaving his Wife and Family Chargeable to the Parish of Henley. Whoever will give such information as may lead to his apprehension, shall receive the above reward.

George Pratt is a shoe maker by trade, and is about six feet high, of a pale complexion, with one side of his chin rather larger than the other, and has a very mild way of speaking, was dressed when he absconded in a blue lapelled coat, trowsers, and white apron, and wore a hat, but sometimes wears a cap ; he was at work in the neighbourhood of Winchester about 18 months ago, and in the neighbourhood of Tamworth about 15 months ago, and was known by the name of " George."

Information to be given to Henry Stephens, Police Officer, Henley-on-Thames.

NICHOLAS MERCER,
Clerk to the Henley Union.

HENLEY-ON-THAMES, }
April 15th, 1842. }

Hampshire Telegraph, 25 April 1842

A particularly unpleasant crime occurred in Henley on 4 September 1843, when 10-year-old Mary Douglas was

---

[92] *HOT Poor Law Union and Workhouse Records 1835 - 1851.* Carol Richmond Oxfordshire Black Sheep Publications 2008.

raped. The offender was John May, aged 46, a bricklayer who in 1841 was an immediate neighbour of John Douglas, a weaver, and his daughter Mary – they lived next door to each other at Pocketts Entry [sic], West Street, Henley-on-Thames. There is no mention of the constable who investigated this case; however, Henry Stephens and Samuel Carter would have been serving at the time. John May had been born in the town on 10 February 1798. His wife Elizabeth nee Bisley had died in May 1843, four months before he was arrested for rape.

May was tried before the Oxfordshire assizes on 11 December 1843. He was arraigned on a charge of violation, stated in the indictment to have been committed upon the person of Mary Douglas, a girl under the age of 10 years. The testimony of the child was reported to be of a more than usually disgusting character, but did not appear to be very conclusive.[93] The report in the *Banbury Guardian* gave more information:

> *John May, a bricklayer aged 41, was indicted for carnally knowing at Henley on Thames, on the 4th October, Mary Douglas, a child under the age of 10 years. The females and boys being ordered out of court, the trial proceeded. Mr. Keating conducted the prosecution. Mary Douglas, the little girl, being the first examined by the learned judge as to the nature of an oath, deposed to the transaction having taken place, in the day time in the privy of the prisoner's house.*

> *The prisoner asserting his innocence, said the child had told a different tale before the magistrates, but he declined asking to have her deposition read, which was suggested to him by the Court. Mr. Young, a surgeon, John Douglas, the child's father, and Mrs. Douglas her step-mother, confirmed her in some of the particulars. The statement of the prisoner before the magistrate,*

[93] Bells New Weekly Messenger 17 December 1843

in which he admitted an assault in his dwelling house, but denying the transaction in the privy, was read. The Jury after two minutes consideration, returned a verdict of guilty, the Judge, in a short but most impressive address to the prisoner, said that until a very recent period, a conviction for such an offence would be followed, not merely by judgment of death, but by execution of that sentence. If anything could raise a question as to the policy of an alteration in the law it would be such a case as this, in which a man advanced in life treats a child in such a manner as might probably lead her in future life to become a prostitute. The law in this case allowed him no discretion, and if it did it would not be one in which he should exercise it, the remainder of prisoner's life would be spent in the most penal settlement of our transport colonies. Sentence, transportation for the term of natural life. A slight attempt at applause was made but immediately suppressed.[94]

John May had previous convictions for poaching and being a deserter, and was transported on the ship *Blundell* on 13 March 1844 to Van Diemen's Land, arriving on 12 July 1844, with 208 other convicts.[95] Today John May would be described as a paedophile and placed on the sex offenders' register. Notwithstanding his punishment for rape, he clearly had not learnt his lesson – on 13 March 1851 he was charged with feloniously assaulting and carnally knowing and abusing Sarah Riley, aged nine, at Hobart. He was tried at Hobart Town Quarter sessions on 5 April 1852 and sentenced to two years' hard labour at Port Arthur Gaol. He was also convicted in April 1856 of 'offences of Misconduct in idling and tippling' and received two months' hard labour. He died in Port Arthur Hospital on 14 January 1865 of disease of the spine.[96]

---

[94] Banbury Guardian 14 December 1843
[95] British Convict Transportation Register State. Library of Queensland.
[96] *Banished. Sentences of Transportation from Oxfordshire Courts.* Carol Richmond. 2007.

Constable Stephens attended Ascot Heath races on Thursday 12 June 1845, although it was not reported whether he was on or off duty. Either way, he went to the assistance of a police colleague, as this newspaper article states:

> *John William Taylor charged with having violently assaulted George Crick in the execution of his duty as constable. George Crick deposed, 'I am a Policeman, and No.40L, of the Metropolitan police force. On the Thursday at Ascot Heath races, it was my duty to separate two men fighting opposite a booth. I went for the purpose, when the defendant came up and struck me a violent blow on my left eye, which caused a black eye. Another policeman came up and attempted to strike the defendant, who then snatched his staff and struck him over the head. He then took the staff away and struck me three violent blows on the head. I have never recovered the effect of the wound, and am now attended by a surgeon'. Henry Stevens, of Henley police force deposed, I was at Ascot Heath. I saw defendant strike Crick on the face when he went up to separate two men fighting. Another officer came up and defendant took away his staff, and struck Crick a tremendous blow on the head, which stunned him. I saw the fight and, that the prisoner Taylor was acting as a second to a man named Maim who was fighting.*
>
> *The Chairman in passing sentence remarked on the violent and improper behaviour of Taylor in committing the assault and also in aiding a fight. Sentence – One year's hard labour.*[97]

Thomas Wordsworth, a labourer of Whitchurch, was found guilty at Oxfordshire Lent Assizes in March 1847 of feloniously breaking into the dwelling house of William

---

[97] *Berkshire Chronicle,* 5 July 1845.

Irons, of Harpsden, and stealing a watch, coat, jacket, waistcoat, trousers, three shirts, six handkerchiefs and other effects worth £3. Constable Stephens and William Reade, a butcher, had gone in search of the offender and found Wordsworth in a public house on the Bath Road. Stephens arrested him and found him in possession of the stolen property. Having also been convicted of a previous felony at Reading quarter sessions in 1845, Wordsworth was sentenced to 15 years' transportation.[98] He had a five-year wait to be transported. On 28 December 1852, he sailed on the ship *St Vincent* from London, arriving at Van Diemen's Land on 26 May 1853 with 213 other convicts.[99] Between 1854 and 1858, Wordsworth was convicted of numerous offences of drunkenness, receiving fines and sentences of imprisonment.

According to his conduct record, Wordsworth's ticket of leave was revoked on 15 March 1859 for being absent, although on 14 February 1863 he was a free man. A ticket of leave allowed convicts to work for themselves on condition that they remained in a specified area, reported regularly to local authorities and, if at all possible, attended worship every Sunday.

By 1848, Constable Henry Stephens was experienced at giving evidence in court as a witness. However, in July of that year Stephens was the defendant in a civil case at the new county court, held in Reading Town Hall, when he appeared before John Billingsley Parry QC. The case was reported as follows:

Langford v Stevens

This was an action of assumpsit*, for the non-payment of the sum of £2 offered as a reward for the apprehension of certain parties, who had committed a felony. Mr. W.

---

[98] *Oxford Chronicle and Reading Gazette,* 13 March 1847.
[99] British Convict Transportation Register. State Library of Queensland.

Bartlett appeared for the plaintiff. The defendant is a police-officer, at Henley-on-Thames, and towards the close of last year a felony was committed on the premises of Mr. Wells in the neighbourhood; the parties were known and they having gone away, a bill was issued giving a description of their persons; a reward of £2 was offered for their apprehension, and information was to be given to the defendant. The plaintiff, who is a carrier, at Assendon, met the prisoners in London and gave the information to Stevens (sic), who promised to pay him the reward if he delivered them into his custody. This the plaintiff did on a subsequent occasion, and the men were committed to gaol for trial. The defendant stated that he had the bills printed by the direction of Mr. Wells, and the reward was to be paid by that party and not by himself.

His Honour said, the presumption that would necessarily arise from reading the printed bill, was, that the defendant was the party by whom the reward was to be paid. There was no other name on it, and, by allowing it to appear, he had made himself liable. Judgement for plaintiff with costs. His Honour, when the case closed, told Stevens, he could recover the amount from Mr Wells, who, if he refused to pay, he recommended should be summoned to appear in this court, and he would make an order for the amount with all the costs.[100]

*The legal term assumpsit, comes from the Latin assumere, meaning 'he undertook.' It refers to a promise made to induce someone to engage in some act, or to pay something to another person. Assumpsit may be made orally, or in writing. Henry Stephens learnt an expensive lesson in this case and it is hoped that he recovered his £2 plus costs, from Mr Wells, without recourse to further civil action.

---

[100] *Reading Mercury*, 29 July 1848.

Most people, if their circumstances allowed, tried to avoid being sent to the workhouse. William Knight, however, decided that he would break into the West Street premises during the evening of 14 May 1850. Knight, aged 60, was spotted by an inmate, William Wood, near a ladder and a broken window. A pile of clothes lay nearby. Wood raised the alarm and Samuel Mortlock, master of the workhouse, was alerted. The clothing found by the ladder was branded with the Union workhouse marks. Knight had discharged himself from the workhouse on the day before Monday 13 July 1850.

Stephens was called. He attended the workhouse at midnight and took Knight into his custody. Knight's explanation for breaking in was an interesting one. In his defence he stated that he had broken into the storeroom, but denied any intention to commit a robbery. His only object was to get transferred from the workhouse, where he had previously been cruelly used, to the gaol, where he felt sure he would be better fed and treated with more kindness and consideration.

At the Oxfordshire summer assizes in July 1850, the Right Honourable Lord Campbell, Lord Chief Justice of her Majesty's Queen's Bench, was not impressed with Knight's defence. He found Knight guilty, and in passing sentence said he was sorry to see a person in his station in life desiring to be pampered with food in a workhouse or a gaol in preference to earning it by his own industry. He assured him, however, that he had made a sad mistake by supposing that he would receive some light sentence, and thus for some few months be enabled to live in a manner satisfactory to himself but without any exertion on his part, and at the expense of the public. He felt it to be his duty to show what an error Knight had committed and, as a warning to others, sentenced him to be transported for seven years.[101]

---

[101] *Oxford Journal,* 20 July 1850.

William Knight was never transported, however; his death was recorded in Portsea in 1853 while he was incarcerated on the hulks.

In the autumn of 1850, Constable Stephens arrested Irishman William Power for assaulting him in the execution of his duty at Henley. Power was fined £4 10 shillings, plus 10 shillings costs; in default, he was committed to gaol for two months.[102]

An easy arrest came Henry Stephens' way when John James, a labourer aged 22 years, walked into the police office on the evening of 24 April 1855 and confessed to arson. A William Brooker had witnessed a pea stack owned by Nathanial Micklem on fire during the evening in the Hop Garden. Another witness, Mary Hollis, had seen James in the afternoon sitting near the pea stack. Ann Gregory also saw him going up the Windmill Field, about 9pm that evening. William Dearlove, bailiff to Mr. Micklem, stated that the burnt pea stack had contained 55 or 60 quarters of peas worth £100. Henry Stephens gave evidence to the Oxfordshire Summer Assizes in July 1855 that James admitted to him that he set fire to the pea stack, giving as a reason that he had not had anything to eat for three days, and perpetrated the act for the purpose of being taken into custody. James had made a written statement to that effect to Stephens, which he then signed, but which he now denied point blank.

Constable Stephens stated in court that the prisoner had explained minutely to the magistrate the manner in which he committed the crime. As a corroboration of the prisoner's first statement, Stephens produced examples of peas, some of which he had found on the prisoner and some from the rick while it was on fire – and they exactly corresponded. At court James denied he had set fire to the rick, and explained his former conduct by stating that he had made the statement

---

[102] *Berkshire Chronicle*, 2 October 1852.

under the impression that it was a good way of getting a night's lodging. He stated that the peas in his possession were from the stack he saw on fire and, being hungry, he took a handful. The jury found James guilty of arson, and the judge, Lord Chief Baron Pollock, in passing sentence said that arson was one of the most mischievous and dangerous offences that could be committed. He further stated that he had no power to pass a shorter sentence, if he sentenced James to transportation, and thought it better to sentence him to transportation rather than penal servitude. The judge believed the sentence, as extended as it might appear, was much better for the prisoner than if he had been sentenced to a shorter period of penal servitude, because he might yet have time for reformation and amendment, as well as a useful career. Sentence: 15 years' transportation.[103] No records can be found of John James being transported to Australia, however.

In March 1855, at the trial of George McDuall and Thomas Wood, (who were both convicted and sentenced to four years' imprisonment, for stealing a coat from Thomas Nathaniel Watts, a clothier of Bell Street, Henley), Stephens, who arrested both men, is referred to in the newspaper report as 'Superintendent'.[104] In another newspaper report two men, William New and Thomas Jones, were tried before Oxford assizes for the theft of a quantity of wheat mixed with peas. Henry Stephens, the arresting officer, gave evidence at their trial and he is named as 'Inspector of Police at Henley'.[105] Whether Stephens gave these ranks himself when giving evidence or the titles were accredited by the newspaper is not known.

Two years later in March 1857 when Oxfordshire Constabulary was formed, Stephens continued as a paid

---

[103] *Banbury Guardian*, 19 July 1855.
[104] *Oxford Chronicle and Reading Gazette*, 10 March 1855.
[105] *Oxford Chronicle and Berks and Bucks Gazette*, 10 March 1855.

parish constable employed by the Henley Corporation. Another two years later, in 1859 he was again appointed by the vestry as parish constable at a salary of £2 per year. The average labourer's wage in 1857 was 10s 8d per week, or just over £28 per annum (see notice below). The small sum of £2 could not have supported Stephens and his family without another income, and he carried on his trade as a carver and gilder at least up until 1861, as this is the occupation recorded in the St Mary's Church baptism register when his youngest daughter Sarah was baptised.

HENLEY.

VESTRY.—At a vestry meeting held on Thursday, the 24th inst., for the purpose of making out a list for the appointment of parish constables, the vestry recommended that Mr. H. Stephens be appointed a paid constable at a salary of £2 per year.

Berkshire Chronicle, Saturday 26 February 1859

Stephens continued to receive respect from the citizens of Henley, as reported in the *Oxford Chronicle* on 1 October 1859, following the annual pleasure fair held in the Market Place on 22 and 23 September.

The newspaper was pleased to announce,

> *That not a case of smashing, picking of pockets, or other serious offence was reported, although numbers of the light-fingered gentry were recognised, which may justly be attributed to the vigilance of our Inspector of Police, Mr Joshua Burton (Oxfordshire Constabulary) and the constables under him, not omitting mention our active constable, Mr Henry Stephens.*

This article clearly shows that Stephens worked closely with those officers of the Oxfordshire Constabulary who were now the primary law enforcement force in Henley-on-Thames.

While he was still an active constable in December 1859, Stephens was assaulted by Francesio Antoin, an Italian who was travelling with an organ. The defendant was told by Stephens to desist playing the organ while in the vicinity of a seriously ill person. Antoin refused to do so and, after further altercation, he struck the constable a severe blow with a stick, which was carried to support the organ. Antoin was found guilty and fined 10 shillings with 8 shillings costs, which were paid by his employer.

In 1860, as well as being the town constable Henry Stephens was also a fireman, as the following newspaper report shows:

On Wednesday 4th January 1860 at 6pm a fire broke out at the farm premises of Mr Longford of Cowfield Farm situated between Henley and Rotherfield Grays, which threatened destruction to a large amount of property. The fire originated in a wheat rick. Mr Longford immediately dispatched a messenger to Henley for the engine and assistance, and in a very short space of time the engine, in charge of Mr Henry Stephens, and vast number of persons were on the spot. Mr John Williams of the Red Lion Inn, Henley, having sent a pair of horses to overtake the engine, which was being drawn there by hand.

The fire was extinguished with the help of the engines from Mr Mackenzie of Fawley Court. The newspaper article continued:

We cannot conclude without remarking that the police were exceedingly active and rendered most valuable assistance.[106]

On 11 March 1860, Stephens arrested Robert Shaw, 78, and John Fitzpatrick, 49, two travelling labourers, for uttering a

---

[106] *Oxford Chronicle and Berks and Bucks Gazette*, 7 January 1860.

counterfeit shilling to Sarah Whatman of Henley.[107] When they were searched eight counterfeit shillings and two counterfeit six-penny pieces were found in possession of Shaw. At the Oxfordshire Easter Quarter Sessions in April, both Shaw and Fitzpatrick were sentenced to six months' imprisonment.[108]

In 1861, Stephens was still living with his family in Albion Place, Henley-on-Thames. Sadly, his wife Sarah died in February 1861 aged 43 years. Sarah's death is most likely to have occurred during or following the birth of her youngest daughter Sarah, who was born in the same month. During their 25-year marriage, Henry and Sarah had 14 children.

Henry Stephens is mentioned in April 1862, when he laid information against Patrick Mckenny, who was charged with deserting from the military train on 3 December 1857. Mckenny, who also gave the name John Sullivan, was committed to gaol to await military escort. Mckenny had deserted from the military (branch unknown) four and a half years previously and remained free until his arrest in April 1862.[109]

Another offender who escaped justice for three years was ex-Henley resident James Powell. Powell, a prolific thief, was arrested in Reading, where he was living in September 1862, by Henley Police Inspector Philip Cope. Powell was charged with breaking into the premises of Mr Joseph Theobald, grocer of Bell Street, Henley-on-Thames, during the early hours of 20 April 1859 and stealing cheese, lard, soap and tobacco.

Powell was seen near the Hop Gardens, carrying a bundle containing the stolen goods, by PC Cousins (Oxfordshire

---

[107] Sarah and her husband William were publicans.
[108] *Berkshire Chronicle*, 16 April 1860.
[109] *South Bucks Free Press Wycombe and Maidenhead Journal*, 11 April 1862.

Constabulary), who gave chase. Powell dropped the bundle and escaped. PC Cousins had recognised Powell, however, and waited outside his house until he returned later that morning. On being confronted, Powell again ran off and although PC Cousins obtained a warrant for Powell's arrest in 1859, Powell evaded arrest until September 1862.

At the September 1862 hearing, Henry Stephens gave evidence to the Henley petty sessions, when he deposed that he was the town sergeant and parish constable and that he had investigated the burglary at Mr Theobald's premises following the break-in in April 1859. Mr Theobald identified to Stephens the goods recovered by PC Cousins as having been stolen during the burglary. William Horsley, the son of William Horsley the 1825 parish constable, gave evidence that he was a pork butcher and could identify the bladder of lard that had been stolen and recovered – he had sold it to Mr Theobald a fortnight before the burglary.

Powell was also charged with another burglary, this time at the premises of his Uncle William Powell, saddler and harness maker of Hart Street, Henley-on-Thames, on 3 September 1862. On this occasion he stole three £5 notes of the Reading Bank, three sovereigns and about £3 in silver coin, seven silver spoons, one pair of silver sugar tongs, one silver-bladed knife and two silver thimbles. James Powell's mother, Charlotte Powell, the sister of the aggrieved William Powell, was charged with receiving a portion of the property despite knowing it had been stolen. Charlotte lodged at the Crown beer house in Duke Street, Henley-on-Thames.[110] James and Charlotte Powell appeared before the Oxfordshire assizes on 2 March 1863. James Powell pleaded guilty to all offences and was gaoled for six years. Charlotte Powell pleaded not guilty to receiving stolen property, was found guilty and, following a plea for clemency from the jury due to the amount of time already spent on remand, she was sentenced to two months' imprisonment.[111]

---

[110] *The South Bucks Free Press, South Oxfordshire Gazette*, 27 September 1862.
[111] *Reading Mercury*, 3 March 1863.

We see from the above case that Henry Stephens was still employed as a town constable in 1862, as well as being the town sergeant. The role of the town sergeant includes civic and ceremonial support to the mayor and the Town Council, and still exists today.

By 1871, Henry Stephens, aged 69 years and no longer a constable, had suffered a severe setback and was in Henley Workhouse as a pauper inmate with five of his children. Was Stephens regarded as a 'de facto' police officer by the master of the workhouse, Mr Samuel Mortlock? Perhaps, for on 6 January 1872 a newspaper report states:

Thomas Stacey, an inmate of the Henley Union Workhouse, was charged with assaulting Samuel Mortlock, the Master of the workhouse on the 2nd instant. Prisoner pleaded not guilty. Samuel Mortlock deposed: 'that on the 2nd inst; complaint was made to him of the prisoner having misconducted himself, and upon enquiry he found that the prisoner had been playing tricks with his gruel, and he accused him of doing so and remonstrated him, upon which the prisoner kicked him and then struck him in the back of the neck with his fist. Prisoner was then taken charge of by Hy. Stephens'. Henry Stephens was then sworn, and he corroborated the evidence of Mr Mortlock. Convicted – Sentenced to 21 days hard labour. The prisoner was then charged with wilfully breaking and damaging a door post of the cell at the Workhouse. Henry Stephens deposed: 'that the prisoner was placed in the cell after committing the assault above mentioned, and shortly afterwards upon visiting cell he found the door post broken and the cell otherwise damaged – he then took off the prisoners' shoes and left him – the damage amounted to 5s'.

Convicted – Sentenced to 14 days hard labour to commence at the expiration of the above term.[112]

---

[112] *Henley Advertiser*, 6 January 1872.

Henry Stephens holds an important place in the history of policing Henley-on-Thames. His career spanned over 25 years as a constable. He was also a fireman and town sergeant. He would have been a readily identifiable figure, known to many of the town's residents over that period. He is named in at least 40 quarter sessions documents that are currently held by the Oxfordshire History Centre. Stephens also has many mentions, including tributes, in local newspaper articles, and was regarded as an active constable who had the respect of the townsfolk. It was unfortunate that the circumstances of his retirement did not afford him a more dignified end to his life. He died in the workhouse on 27 January 1879 aged 74 years. The cause of death was certified as 'paralysis one year'. His pauper funeral was held on 31 January at St Mary's Church, Henley-on-Thames. Henry Stephens is interred at the Fairmile Cemetery in a pauper's grave in section 3, plot 193. No gravestone marks his resting place.[113]

Section 3 of Henley Cemetery looking towards the chapel.
Authors collection.

---

[113] Henley Town Council Cemetery Records.

John WICHELO/WHICHELO/WICKELOW

Wichelo was a Henley constable from 1836 to 1838, and possibly longer having previously been a labourer. He married Ann Perrin on 24 November 1833 at St Mary's Church, Henley-on-Thames. They had three children, John, Ann and Mary. John's occupation is recorded in the St Mary's Church baptism register as 'policeman' in 1836 and 1839 on the baptism of his children.

Official court documents also record him as a constable from 1836, when he gave evidence in the following case of larceny. Sarah Brown, the wife of Richard Brown, was charged in April 1836 with stealing four towels and two sacks, the property of Thomas Lawrence of Henley-on-Thames. Wichelo was the arresting officer.[114]

In July 1837, Wichelo arrested Samuel Jemmett, William Jemmett, William Trimmings and Henry Foster, who were tried at the county quarter sessions for the theft of a quantity of bacon from Elizabeth Reeves of Shiplake. Samuel Jemmett was found guilty and sentenced to three months' imprisonment. The other three were acquitted.[115]

In August 1838, Constable John Whichelo charged James Langford with stealing one truss of Sanfoin hay from Thomas Beesley of Henley-on-Thames.[116] However, no outcome of this case has been found.

There is a record of the burial of a John Wichelo who died in January 1840, aged 39 years, in St Mary's Church burial register. It is possible that John died while he was still serving as a constable, although there is no documentary evidence to confirm this. His death was just three months after the birth of his daughter Mary, who was born in

---

[114] *Oxford Journal*, 16 April 1836.
[115] *Oxford Chronicle and Reading Gazette*, 1 July 1857.
[116] *Oxford Chronicle and Reading Gazette*, 18 August 1838.

October 1839. John's widow Ann gave birth to an illegitimate son, Charles Witcheloe, in October 1843. Charles' father is not named in the baptism register.

Samuel CARTER

Records show that the next town constable after John Wichelo was Samuel Carter. Samuel was born in Henley-on-Thames, on 27 July 1796 to Thomas Carter and Deborah nee Cooper.

Samuel was a constable from 1841 to 1845. In the 1841 census, Carters age is given as 40 years and he living in Northfield End with his wife Rebecca nee Iveoby. His occupation is given on this census form as 'police'. Sadly, Rebecca had only days to live. The 1841 census was taken on the night of Sunday 6 June 1841, and Rebecca's funeral was held 11 days later, on 17 June at St Mary's Church; she was 33 years old.

In July 1841 Constable Carter gave evidence at the Berkshire assizes held in Abingdon, in the case of the murder of Henry Street, at Wargrave, Berks. The defendant in this case was George Tyson, who had broken into the home of a farmer, Mr Adams, and threatened to blow the brains of any man who entered the premises. Henry Street tried to secure Tyson and was shot by him. The night before, Tyson had asked Constable Carter if he could spend the night in the Henley lock-up, which he had been allowed to do. At 9 the next morning when Carter unlocked the cage, Tyson ran out without his shoes and waistcoat 'in a state of alarm', shouting that there had been five or six men standing over him with drawn knives. Constable Carter believed that Tyson was labouring under some delusion, given that he had been alone in the lock-up. Tyson was subsequently acquitted of murder by the jury on the grounds of his 'disordered state of mind'.[117]

---

[117] *Reading Mercury*, 17 July 1841.

Tyson was detained to Reading Gaol to await a decision over his fate, and while he was there, he manifested 'symptoms of insanity'. On Saturday 23 April 1842, Tyson hanged himself in his cell by tying his bed linen to the window shutter. He was 35 years old.[118,119]

On 27 July 1841, Constable Carter arrested Richard Lewendon and John Harpur, and charged them with stealing two geese from George Strange, of Henley-on-Thames. They were both committed to the county gaol.

Samuel Carter remarried in Reading, Berks, towards the end of 1841. He and his second wife, Jane Stanbridge, had two children, Frederick Henry and James William. His policing career apparently lasted until 1845 – his occupation is recorded as constable when their son James William was baptised at St Mary's Church, Henley-on-Thames, on 1 August 1845. There is no further record of him serving after this date. He died in April 1847 aged 49 years. Jane died a year later in March 1848.

Benjamin SMITH

One record lists a Benjamin Smith as constable in 1845, when his name appears in a list of fines and penalties from the Henley division for neglecting his duty as a constable. No details of his neglect are recorded. There is no certainty that Benjamin Smith was a constable in the town; only that he was a constable in the Henley petty sessional area, which could be any of the parishes surrounding Henley.

Joseph BALLARD

In 1848 Joseph Ballard is first recorded as a constable; he served for five years until he was dismissed in 1853. Born in Caversham, Oxon, Ballard lived with his wife Elizabeth in

---

[118] Berkshire Burial Index.
[119] *Reading Mercury*, 30 April 1842.

Bell Street, Henley, and is listed as a police officer in the 1851 census and in several quarter sessions records and newspaper articles.

On 10 April 1848, 12-year-old James M'Quhae was returning home from school when he was stopped by two men on Henley Hill, not far from the toll bar. They grabbed him and searched his pockets, taking 2 pence, all the money he possessed. The boy reported the theft and Joseph Ballard investigated. A witness, Lovell, had seen the men on the road just before the robbery was committed and was able to give a description of them. That same evening, Ballard arrested John Fitzgibbons, 21, and Edward Jones, 25, in a Henley lodging house. Both men were convicted at the Berkshire Midsummer Quarter Sessions in July 1848, and sentenced to six months' hard labour.[120]

On 3 August 1852, Constable Ballard stopped and searched John Dyer, an Irish navvy, who was found in possession of 16 and a half yards of cloth. When questioned, Dyer said it was his property. Ballard took Dyer into custody and his enquiries found that the cloth had been stolen from the shop window of Mr Thomas Nathaniel Watts, a tailor of Bell Street, Henley-on-Thames. At the Oxfordshire Michaelmas Quarter Sessions, Dyer was found guilty and sentenced to six months' hard labour.

One recorded case heard at Oxfordshire assizes was a case of grievous bodily harm with intent by Joseph Barney, aged 51 years, who stabbed John Carter in Hart Street, Henley, in 1853. Ballard gave evidence as the arresting officer. Barney was found guilty and was sentenced to 18 months' imprisonment with hard labour.

---

[120] *Reading Mercury*, 1 July 1848.

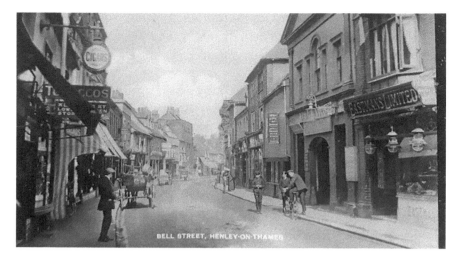

Bell Street, Henley-on-Thames. Author's collection
The Minster Real Photo Series Postcard.

At the quarter sessions in July 1853, Ballard was the arresting officer in a case against another Carter – this time William Carter, 17 – and George Douglas, 16, who were charged with stealing 24lb of lead from Joseph Partridge and the Rev. T.B. Morrell of Henley-on-Thames. Carter was found guilty and sentenced to six months' imprisonment. Douglas was acquitted.[121]

In 1851 Joseph Ballard's and Henry Stephen's tenure as police constables coincided with the introduction in Oxfordshire of the post of superintending constables, which is explained in chapter six.

Constable Ballard's career came to an ignominious end on Monday 19 September 1853, as this newspaper article reports:

Dismissal of a Police Officer

A meeting of the Magistrates was held at the Town's Clerk's office at the beginning of the week, for the

---

[121] *Oxford University and City Herald*, 2 July 1853.

purpose of investigating a charge of indecent assault on a female, alleged to have been committed by police constable Joseph Ballard, during the previous midnight, when on his beat. Their worships after due consideration, and hearing the evidence adduced, came to a resolution, the effect of which was his immediate dismissal.[122]

Apart from the disciplinary investigation held by the magistrates, described above, there was no court case and the details of these serious allegations are not recorded. Although Ballard's employment as a constable in Henley was over, this was not the end of his police career. He continued to work as a police officer, as a constable of the West India Dock Police at Blackwall Basin in East London. Unfortunately for Ballard, tragedy was to strike on 2 October 1855, as reported in the *Morning Chronicle*:

One of the officers of the West India Dock Police, named Ballard, has been discovered drowned in the Blackwall Basin, having, it is supposed, fallen overboard while returning from the ship 'Samuel', which he had boarded to see that the lights were out, in accordance with the dock regulations.

Further information is given in the *Oxford Chronicle* on 20 October 1855:

Mr Joseph Ballard, late police officer of this town (Henley) and since employed in one of the docks in London as policeman, was drowned on Tuesday night. It is supposed that whilst walking along the side of the basin he fell in, his hat was found floating. His body was not found for several days after.

Ballard was 49 years old when he died. His wife Elizabeth continued to live in Henley as a lodging house keeper in

---

[122] *Reading Mercury*, 24 September 1853.

Hart Street, although it is not known if Joseph Ballard still lived with her in Henley at the time of his death.

Thomas BOLTON

Records show Thomas Bolton was a night watchman in 1853 and was a constable from 1854 to 1857. Bolton was born on 4 November 1811 in the town. In the 1841 census, he was a shoemaker living in West Street, Henley, with his wife Elizabeth and two daughters. They had a total of nine children between 1841 and 1854.

Thomas Bolton is named as a night watchman[123] in October 1853, in the case of William Webb and John Sadler, both of Rotherfield Grays, who were convicted of stealing two beech spokes from their master, James Wheeler. Webb was given two months' imprisonment and Sadler was to be whipped and discharged.[124]

David MacDonald, John Barnes, William Jones and James Harris were arrested by Bolton for breaking into a shop and stealing watches from Charles R. Palmer, silversmith, in February 1854. At Oxfordshire quarter sessions MacDonald was acquitted; the other three defendants were sentenced to four years' imprisonment.[125]

Thomas Bolton obtained a conviction against Elizabeth Meades, who was fined 9 shillings and 3 pence for stealing turnips from J.H. Wilson, of Peppard, in April 1854.[126]

In the same month Constable Bolton arrested George Smith and George Williams, both of Henley-on-Thames, for theft of a cloth coat from James Talbot of Market Place. Both were sentenced to two months' hard labour at the quarter sessions in June 1854.[127]

---

[123] OHC QS1853/4/L2/66.
[124] *Reading Chronicle*, 22 October 1853.
[125] Oxford University & City Herald 4 March 1854.
[126] OHC. QS 1854/4/L2/2.
[127] *Oxford Journal*, 22 April 1854.

On 7 August 1854, Thomas Bolton gave evidence at the inquest at the White Horse and Star Inn, Henley-on-Thames, before the coroner J.H. Cooke, on the body of Eliza Hood, aged 53, who was found drowned the previous morning in the River Thames. Hood had lodged with Charlotte and Thomas Owen, a shoemaker, in Hog Lane, Northfield End. Mrs Owen deposed that she had lived with them for about 12 months and had a strange manner. Hood had gone out for a walk alone the previous evening along the Marlow Road and had not returned by 10pm. Her body was found early the next morning, lying face down in the water, about 15 feet from the bank by Mr William Foster and his son. Thomas Bolton helped remove the body from the river and take her to the kitchen of Mr and Mrs Owen. The verdict was: 'Found drowned, but how she came into the water there was no evidence.'[128]

In the same month, Constable Bolton gave evidence at Reading magistrates' court, in the case of assault on John Johnson, son of the lock-keeper at Blake's Pound. The defendants, were Thomas Thorpe Junior, William Norris and William Rose, all of Henley. Rose, a bricklayer, failed to attend the hearing and Bolton proved to the court that he had serviced the summons on him. Thorpe and Rose were found guilty; Norris was acquitted. Thorpe was fined £2 10 shillings and costs of £1 2s 6d, and in default of immediate payment was committed to the county gaol for one month. The wife of Rose was at the hearing and apologised for her husband's absence and begged time for payment. The bench ordered him to appear in a week and pay his fine or a warrant would be issued for his arrest in default.[129]

Bolton arrested Charles Sparks for stealing 50lb of beech wood from his master, James Wheeler of Henley-on-Thames, on 13 December 1854. Sparks was sentenced to four months' hard labour in January 1855 at Oxfordshire quarter sessions.

---

[128] *Banbury Guardian*, 10 August 1854.
[129] *Reading Mercury*, 19 August 1854.

At 3pm on 12 February 1855, Henry Morgan, 28, and Thomas Jones, 37, were seen by shopman Thomas N. Watts taking a pair of boots from his shop and running away down Bell Street, Henley. Mr Watts hailed a lad and they gave chase and managed to catch the thieves, with the property in their possession. They handed them into the custody of Bolton the constable. The prisoners' defence was that they had seen the boots lying on the pavement and took them down the street with the intention of giving them to the first police constable they met. On March 6 at Oxfordshire assizes, Morgan and Jones were both convicted and sentenced to four years' penal servitude.[130]

Constable Bolton also gave evidence at another inquest, this time into the death of William Piercey of the Fair Mile, Henley, in February 1855. Bolton deposed that Piercey was found on the Mount at the rear of his residence with his throat cut and a razor in his right hand. The coroner J.H. Cooke recorded a verdict of suicide while suffering from temporary insanity.[131]

On 15 January 1855, Constable Bolton arrested George Evans and William Johnson, both labourers, for breaking a window and stealing 7lb of pork from the shop of Joseph Pepjoy, in Bell Street, Henley. On searching them, Bolton recovered several pieces of pork. Johnson, aged 19 years, was sentenced to four years' penal servitude and Evans to 18 months' imprisonment with hard labour.

A year later on 25 February 1856, Constable Thomas Bolton's wife Elizabeth died aged 43, after what was described as 'six years severe affliction'.[132]

Finally, Thomas Bolton is mentioned in a newspaper report in May 1857 as having charged Samuel Lambourne, of

[130] *Reading Mercury*, 10 March 1855.
[131] *Reading Mercury*, 17 February 1855.
[132] *Reading Mercury*, 8 March 1856.

Henley, with having damaged some grass growing in a meadow near the Thames in the parish of Fawley, the property of E. Mackenzie; and with doing the same in the parish of Hambleden on the property of E. Majoribanks. Lambourne was fined for damage 1 shilling in each case, and 5 shillings costs.[133]

Henry Stephens and Thomas Bolton were the final two paid town constables to police Henley before the formation of the Oxfordshire Constabulary in 1857.

---

[133] *Reading Mercury*, 9 May 1857.

Chapter Six

Superintending Constables Act 1850

This legislation provided for a superintendent constable to be appointed for each petty sessional division of a county by the quarter sessions, and was adopted by Oxfordshire in 1850. Paid out of the county rate, these men reported to the petty sessions magistrates. The superintending constable's duties would involve overseeing the work of the parish constables in the division, as well as being responsible for the lock-ups in the area. However, the superintendent constable had no power to appoint or dismiss any of the parish constables in his division. That was in the control of the justices.

Parish constables did not figure highly in the opinion of the Banbury superintending constable, David **SMITH**, who had previously been a member of the Essex Constabulary. In evidence to a parliamentary select committee on policing in 1853, Smith stated 'that half a dozen regular Essex policemen would be equal to the seventy parish constables now under me'.

Many of the superintending constables who were hired were professional police officers and had been employed in established police forces before their transfer into this new role. In February 1851 an advertisement appeared in provincial newspapers for the office of superintendent constable for the petty sessional division of Henley.

Matthew MORAN

Twenty people applied for the position. At a sitting of the Oxfordshire adjourned quarter sessions on Saturday

9 March 1851, Lord Camoys proposed, and Mr Powys seconded, that a Matthew Moran, who used to work for the London Police and had recently been employed at Broadwindsor in Dorset as a police constable, be appointed superintendent for the Henley division. The proposition was carried unanimously. Moran's salary was £105 per year, and he had to provide a horse and cart, and perform similar duties and be subject to the same regulations as the superintending constables recently appointed for other Oxfordshire divisions.

POLICE.

WANTED,—A Person for the Office of SUPERINTENDING CONSTABLE of the Hen-ury Petty Sessional Division within the County of Oxford (to be appointed under the 13th Victoria, cap. 20). He must be experienced in the duties of a Police Officer, and be able to read and write well, and to keep accounts. The salary will be One Hundred and Five Pounds per annum ; and he will have to provide himself with Clothes, Lodgings, and a Horse and Cart. The County will provide the requisite Books and Stationery, but nothing else in addition to the salary.

Written applications, with full particulars, age, &c., and accompanied by testimonials, to be sent to the under-signed, at the County Hall, Oxford, on or before the First of March next.

JOHN M. DAVENPORT,
Clerk of the Peace of the County of Oxford.
10th February 1851.

Superintending constable advert. *Oxford University, City and County Herald*, 15 February 1851

In 1851 the Henley petty sessional division comprised the hundreds of Binfield and Langtree and part of the hundred of Dorchester, including the parishes of Bix, Caversham, Checkendon, Crowmarsh Gifford, Eye and Dunsden, Goring, Harpsden, Henley-on-Thames, Ipsden, Mapledurham, Mongewell, Nuneham Murren, Northstoke, Rotherfield Greys, Rotherfield Peppard, Shiplake, Southstoke with Woodcote and Whitchurch.

Ten years earlier Matthew Moran, an Irishman born in Waterford, aged 34, in 1841 was living with his wife Caroline and son Matthew in Little Queen Street, in the parish of St Margaret, Westminster, London, and was a serving police officer in the Metropolitan Police.

Also notable in his past was a case that Matthew Moran investigated in November 1848 in Dorset, which was reported in the *Dorset Chronicle*.[134] At an inquest at Broadwinsor on the deaths of John Hoare aged six months and William Hoare aged three years, the sons of dairyman John Hoare, it was stated that Matthew Symes a baker and beer house keeper had illegally inoculated the two children for the smallpox, which resulted in their deaths. Constable Moran had previously summoned Symes, who appeared before magistrates at Bridport for illegally inoculating smallpox in six cases even though Moran had previously cautioned him not to. Symes on that occasion had been sentenced to six months' imprisonment. Moran's evidence at the coroner's court led to Symes being found guilty and indicted for manslaughter by the jurors.

Following his appointment as superintending constable for the petty sessions division of Henley, Moran moved with the permission of the justices to the village of Whitchurch with his wife and now five children. He would at this point have been the supervisor of Constables Stephens and Ballard at Henley as well as other constables in the parishes that comprised the petty sessions division.

In May 1851, it was announced in the local newspapers that Moran and other superintending constables in other divisions had been appointed as the inspector of weights and measures for the Henley petty sessional division. One of Moran's responsibilities was to ensure shopkeepers and other sellers had scales and weights that were correctly

---

[134] *The Dorset County Chronicle and Somersetshire Gazette*, 16 November 1848.

calibrated and that goods sold were of the correct weight. Many prosecutions were brought for offences under the Weights and Measures Act.

Just a few months into his role as superintending constable, Moran was himself to become a victim of crime. On 12 July 1851 Martha Willis, aged 19, who was employed as a servant at the Moran's family home, was arrested for stealing two brooches worth 3s, a gold pin worth 2s 6d and an apron worth 6d, all the property of Caroline Moran. At her trial in October 1851, at the Oxfordshire quarter sessions, she pleaded not guilty. It was heard that Willis had been in service for about two months before being dismissed as a result of information received. Moran went to see Willis at her father's house on 20 July and saw that Willis was wearing the stolen apron and had one of the stolen brooches on her chest. In her bedroom Moran found the second brooch and the gold pin was found in the apron. All of the items were identified by Mrs Caroline Moran as her property. In her defence Willis stated that she did not steal the items but found them. The jury found her guilty of larceny. The chairman of the bench, the Reverend A.H. Matthews, stated that it was 'a very wretched thing to see a young woman standing a convicted criminal in a court of justice and that her crime was much increased by the breach of trust of which she had been found guilty'. Willis was sentenced to four months' imprisonment with hard labour.[135]

Matthew Moran was regularly mentioned as a witness in the local newspapers, prosecuting cases at petty and quarter sessions as superintending constable. In January 1852 he gave evidence against a Jesse Druce of Southstoke, for stealing a ewe from Thomas Clare. Moran had searched Druce's home and found the carcass of a sheep in a cupboard under the stairs. Thomas Clare identified the marks on the sheep skin as those of his ewe. Druce was found guilty and sentenced to nine months' hard labour.

---

[135] *Oxford Chronicle and Berks and Bucks Gazette,* 18 October 1851.

Not all ratepayers were impressed with the Henley superintending constable, though, as a letter in 1852 to the *Reading Mercury* showed:

Sir,

Some time since a Superintending Constable was appointed to the Henley Division. I do not know what the duties of a Superintending Constable may be, but this I do know, that the parish constables though generally willing to do their duty, rarely know how to set about. I therefore supposed that this Superintendent was to be in frequent communication with them, to give them instruction, and to receive from them information on various matters, but I suppose I am in error, for the Magistrates have placed him amongst the beech woods at Stoke Row, where there is the least population, and from knowledge of the division, the man is at the greatest distance he could possibly be from all the populous places in it, with bad roads, or no roads and so far from being easily got at, it would be a good day's work for any constable to go to him from most of the parishes from the division.

Whoever knows anything of this district must know that Henley itself is at the extreme corner of the county and of the division bounded on two sides out of three by Berkshire and Bucks, and whoever like myself has served parish offices, must know to his cost that Henley is perhaps the most inconvenient petty sessional division in this or any other county.

Most of the parishes are ten miles distant, whilst more than two-thirds of the division attend Reading or Wallingford markets, so that when called to Henley, they have not, as in most other districts, any other business calling them there on market day.

Any person with any knowledge of this division would fix upon some spot between Caversham and Crowmarsh as the most assessable and central point; and I would find two or three spots near which good roads branch off to Goring, Whitchurch and all the villages on the river; also, to Nettlebed and Henley, and it is exactly on these roads where an intelligent officer might intercept the sheep and fowl-stealers, all of whom carry off their booty across the river. Now, Sir, whether I am right or wrong in these observations, the proof of the pudding is in the eating, but at present the rogues continue to eat our sheep, turkeys and chickens &c, &c, with impunity. The county put, one way or other, to the expense of 150l. a year at least, as I hear; and I have not heard of one thief being detected, except the superintending constable's own servant. Neither is crime prevented, as I hear of continued fowl and sheep-stealing, to say nothing of petty pilfering. Allow me to suggest to my fellow rate-payers, to forward to you, Sir, information of every robbery that takes place and then I think if you do not report also some cases of detection, the rate-payers will demur to the continuance of so fruitless an expense.

I am Sir, your humble servant. A County Rate-Payer.

P.S. Since writing of the above, I have heard of the detection and conviction of one sheep-stealer from South Stoke, but from what I hear, the theft was so clumsily managed, that the parish constable unassisted could not have failed in detecting it.[136]

However, although it seems that some in the county were not impressed with the location of Moran's lodgings or his efficiency, it was the justices that he had to justify his efforts to. Each quarter, he was required to submit returns on the duties he performed as superintending constable to the Oxfordshire quarter sessions.

On 14 October 1852 Moran submitted his Michaelmas report to 'Her Majesty's Justices of the Peace at Quarter

---

[136] Reading Mercury, 17 January 1852.

93

Sessions, County of Oxford'. This rare surviving report for the period between the Trinity and Michaelmas Sessions provides the following information and a useful insight into his duties:[137]

> *Gentlemen*
>
> *I must respectfully beg leave to report the state of the Division as being very quiet. The Magistrates has had several cases at Petty Sessions such as Bastardy, assaults and two or three cases of Poaching – but no crime of consequence, there has not been one person committed for trial during the Quarter. The printed form of report will show you the number of Public and beer houses I have summoned to the Petty Sessions – namely 2 public houses and 5 beer shops on which convictions were obtained except on two. I beg leave to state as regards the Constables that a very good feeling exists between them and me as regards duty affairs in giving them orders, or instructions, they obey me with respect, not the slightest hesitation in doing anything I require of them. The Weights and Measures Inspector of the Watlington Division has had them this quarter, the Adjuster has adjusted some weights in the Division but in consequence of not having the Standard weights to prove them by I have not stamped them. I have taken the advantage while passing through the Division to examine the scales.*
>
> *Matthew Moran*
> *Superintending Constable, Henley Division*

---

[137] Oxfordshire History Centre OHC QS/1852/4/A8/10.

Copy of Matthew Moran's superintending
constable's expenses of 1852.[138]

It would appear that Moran was not as dissatisfied with the constables of the Henley division as others were.

The printed form that Moran submitted with his report contains the following information on individuals prosecuted for licensing offences.

1. *Thomas Goodchild. Publican, Parish of Eye & Dunsden. On the 8th July 1852 having his (Public) house open during afternoon service. Fined One pound with Ten Shillings costs – Paid. Information laid by the Superintending Constable.*

2. *Abraham Richards. Beer House, Parish of Rotherfield Greys. On 8th July 1852 having his house open after ten o'clock PM. Two cases one night after the other. Fined Four pounds with One Pound costs – Paid. Information laid by the Superintending Constable.*

---

[138] Oxfordshire History Centre. QS1852/4/FS 16

Richards probably committed these offences as a beer seller while living at the Gas Tap, at 69 Greys Road – he is recorded at the address in the 1851 census with his wife Sarah. He was also employed as a Coachsmith.[139]

> 3. *James Wilder. Beer House, Parish of Rotherfield Greys. On 8th July 1852 having his house open after ten o'clock PM. Case dismissed. Information laid by the Superintending Constable.*

James Wilder was the landlord of the Anchor pub, Friday Street, from 1850 to 1868.[140] He was also a bricklayer and married to Elizabeth.

> 4. *William Turner. Beer House, Parish of Caversham. On 22nd July 1852 having his house open after ten o'clock PM. Fined Ten Shillings with One Pound Twelve Shillings and Six Pence costs – Paid. Information laid by Edward Bells Parish Constable.*
> 5. *James Butler. Beer House, Parish of North Stoke. On 5th August 1852 having his house open after Ten o'clock PM. Fined One Pound. Information laid by the Superintending Constable.*

In the 1851 census James Butler, aged 50 years, whose occupation was given as publican, was living with his wife Hannah.

> 6. *Daniel Wells. Beer House, Parish of Caversham. On 5th August 1852 having his house open after Ten o'clock PM. Fined Ten Shillings with Ten Shillings costs – Paid. Information laid by Edward Bells Parish Constable.*

---

[139] *The Hostelries of Henley.* Ann Cottingham 2000.
[140] Ibid.

> 7. *John Lovejoy. Publican, Parish of Henley. On 16th September 1852 for having his house open during afternoon service. Fined Ten Shillings with Ten Shillings costs – Paid. Information laid by the Superintending Constable.*

John Lovejoy, aged 51, is recorded in the 1851 census as a licensed victualler living in Northfield End with his wife Mary. He was the landlord of the Hope Public House between 1851 and 1854.[141]

> 8. *Joseph Button. Beer House, Parish of Henley. On 16th September 1852 for having his house open during afternoon service. Case dismissed. Information laid by the Superintending Constable.*

Joseph Button's occupation in 1851 is recorded as a sawyer and he is shown to be lodging with 46-year-old widow Sarah Hemmings, a beer house keeper, in Northfield End. *The Hostelries of Henley* records that this was the Windsor Castle Public House; presumably Joseph Button took over from Sarah Hemmings, given that he was the subject of the information laid by Matthew Moran.

The superintending constables' returns were countersigned by Charles Lane, chairman of the justices of the peace. Matthew Moran also submitted his claim for expenses of two shillings and 10 pence for stamps and information to the clerk of the peace, Mr M. Davenport, between the Trinity and Michaelmas Sessions.

At the meeting of the Oxfordshire Michaelmas Sessions held on 18 October 1852 it was reported that:

---

[141] Ibid.

Henley Division

The duties of the Superintending Constable have been satisfactorily performed, the books properly kept, and his return as Superintending Constable correctly made. No duties have been performed by him during the past quarter as Inspector of weights and measures.[142]

At another quarter sessions meeting held in January 1853 Moran's attitude towards his constables had clearly changed, as a newspaper report of the meeting states:

Henley Division

The Superintendent Constable complains with apparent justice, of the habitual omission of a majority of the Parish Constables to initiate any enquiries into crime reported to have been committed in their locality, although willing to assist in the detection of it when called into requisition by the Superintending Constable.[143]

This complaint appears to have been a common problem among parish constables in the county, as the clerk to the quarter sessions at the same meeting read out a joint report from the superintendents stating:

The Superintending Constables frequently experience an indifference on the part of the Parochial Constables to render that prompt aid in the detection of crime which their local knowledge or proximity to the scene of an offence, might render of conclusive importance, and with a view not only of reminding the Parish Constables of their duties as officers of the police, but by enforcing a performance of those duties if they should hereafter neglect them.

---

[142] *Oxford Chronicle and Berks & Bucks Gazette,* 23 October 1852.
[143] *City and County Advertiser,* 8 January 1853.

The committee recommended that an order be issued from the magistrates in quarter sessions calling the attention of parish constables to their obligations in the first instance, as themselves detective and ministerial officers, and next as bound to cooperate with and to assist the superintending constables. This was a common complaint against parish constables and not only in Oxfordshire.

In April 1853 Moran was less diligent in his returns to the Easter Quarter Sessions, as a newspaper report states that:

Henley Division

There are daily entries in the Superintending Constables diary of his being engaged in his duties. But the quarter's report has not been verified by the counter-signature of Magistrates of the division, as is prescribed. There have been six committals for trial during the quarter, and a conviction ensued in five of the cases. There have also been three summary convictions for miscellaneous offences. As Inspector of weights and measures, he has received 2s 9d for fees, and has not had occasion to lay any information. In addition to salary there is a bill due for payments amounting to 6s. And there is a bill presented by John Tomlinson for assisting the inspector, but it has not been verified by the magistrates of the division.[144]

The same newspaper also reports on the various negotiations for divisional lock-up houses in the county.

For the Henley division it was decided that it would be expedient for the county to take a lease for the term of 21 years, from the Corporation of Henley-on-Thames, for a lock-up house and constable's residence proposed to be built in accordance with a plan that had been prepared by

---

[144] *Oxford Chronicle and Berks & Bucks Gazette*, 9 April 1853.

Mr Buckler the county architect. The terms of the tenancy would be a rent of £21 per annum. The building would include two cells and one room for public purposes and would 'at all times be ready for occupation by prisoners (and constables having care of them) committed by any magistrate of the county'. The cells and rooms would be heated during the winter at the lessee's expense and the rooms would be furnished only to the extent of what was necessary for the object in question, also at the lessee's expense.[145]

The new lock-up house, situated behind the old town hall, was officially opened on 25 March 1854. In a report to the quarter sessions dated 30 March 1854 the Henley magistrates reported the following:

> *We beg to report that the Lockup House at Henley on Thames, provided and built by the Corporation of Henley, with two cells and a house adjoining for the residence of the police constable is completed, with appropriate beds and fittings, and having inspected the same, we find that it is fit for use, and is furnished with every proper requisite. We therefore recommend that the rent to be paid by the County should commence from Lady Day last, the 25th instant.*[146]
>
> *Signed:*
>
> *Thomas Barker*
> *Charles Lane*
> H.P. Powys
> Wm Vanderstyne
> H. Baskerville
> Joseph Henry Wilson

---

[145] Ibid.
[146] OHC. QS/1854/2/A8/15.

Henley lock-up and constable's residence leased from
Henley Corporation and situated behind the Guildhall. It was
demolished when the current town hall was built in 1900.[147]

Also raised at the Easter Quarter Sessions in 1853 was the
question of the superintending constables' pay. All 10 of
the Oxfordshire superintending constables had petitioned
the quarter sessions for a raise in their annual salary and
included payments made to superintendent constables in
other counties. The newspaper article below gives the details.

---

[147] Postcard G. Bushell & Sons

SALARIES OF THE SUPERINTENDING CONSTABLES.

The Clerk of the Peace read the following petition from the Superintending Constables :—

To the Justices of the Peace acting in and for the County of Oxford in Quarter Sessions assembled.

The humble petition of the superintending constables appointed for the several Petty Sessional Divisions in the County of Oxford,

Sheweth,—That the pay allowed to your petitioners has been found by them, after the necessary outfit and expenses connected with their duties in travelling, very inadequate to the support of themselves and families in a way suited to their position, as will appear by the statement hereunto annexed, marked A. That the pay of your petitioners is much below the wages allowed in other counties, to superintending constables. That your petitioners feel assured that they have only to bring their case fully and fairly before you in order to their condition being improved; and in order to this, your petitioners have procured statistics from various counties (without any selection) shewing the rate of wages paid to superintending constables therein, a statement from which your petitioners humbly submit to your notice, in the schedule hereinto annexed, marked B, in the hope that you will resolve to place them on an average footing with the superintending constables referred to. Your petitioners therefore humbly pray you to give their case a just and merciful consideration, and adopt such remedial measures as to you may seem expedient. And as in duty bound, your petitioners will ever pray.

Signed, DAVID SMITH, Supt. Chadlington Division.
R. MITCHELL, Bampton East.
JOHN BARTON, Banbury and Bloxham.
J. W. SMITH, Watlington.
MATTHEW MORAN, Henley Division.
DANIEL HARWOOD, Wootton, North.
ROBT. HITCHMAN, Bullingdon.
THOS. MOULDEN, Ploughley.
JAS. EDMONDS, Wootton South.
WM. MASSEY, Bampton West.

The following is an abstract of the schedule referred to :—

(A) Income and expenditure of the superintending constables of the Oxford Divisions:—Income, £110 ; expenditure, £56 4s. ; balance remaining for support of officers' wife and children, £53 16s.

(B) Statement showing the rate of wages paid to superintending constables in other counties:—

Kent, £150, in addition to £30 for the supply of cart and harness.

Buckinghamshire, £120, half fines, weights and measures, say £5 ; half fees ditto, say £5 ; cart harness and uniform found, say £7 ; total £137.

York, £160 (no other allowance.)

Essex, first-class, £148 18s. ; second class, £138 18s. ; third class, £128 18s. In addition, horse, cart, harness, repairs and uniform found.

Lancashire, £200, and after 3 years service an advance of £30 per annum, and after 7 years a further rise of £20 per annum.

Northampton, £150, including allowance.

Lincolnshire, £140, and in addition, horse, cart, repairs, and harness found.

Oxford Chronicle & Berks and Bucks Gazette, 9 April 1853

102

However, Matthew Moran decided that he would not wait for an increase in his salary, and in June 1853 he submitted his resignation to the justices. Moran left Oxfordshire to take up the position of superintendent and chief officer of Barnstaple Borough Police, Devon, in 1854. He remained there for eight years until his retirement in 1862. Moran then returned to London, and at the age of 66 years was living with his son Matthew, a dentist, at 362 Old Kent Road, Camberwell. In the 1871 census he gives his occupation as retired superintendent of police. Three years later he had moved to the Hertford area, where he died aged 69 years.

Francis KNOCK

Following Moran's resignation in June 1853, the magistrates at Henley petty sessions examined 21 testimonials of prospective candidates for his replacement. After interviewing several of the candidates, the magistrates requested the Oxfordshire quarter sessions to confirm their preferred choice, Francis Knock of Sandon, Essex, be appointed.

At the July quarter sessions Mr P. Powys nominated Francis Knock who, he said, had been an inspector in the Essex Constabulary for 10 years. Mr Charles Lane seconded the nomination, which was at once agreed to.[148]

Essex Police had been formed in 1840 and Francis Knock, who was born in Kent, had left his job as a clerk in April 1840 at the age of 24 and joined as constable number 44.[149] In 1841 he is shown on the census living in Billericay, now an inspector of police, with his wife Amelia and two young daughters. In 1851 he held the rank of superintendent, living at Purleigh Police Station, Essex, with his wife and now seven children. He was also a qualified weights and measures inspector for Essex Police.

---

[148] *Oxford Chronicle and Berks and Bucks Gazette*, 2 July 1853.
[149] *Sworn to Serve. Police in Essex*, Maureen Scollan. Phillimore & Co. 1993.

On his appointment to the Henley division, Knock moved with his family to the village of Checkendon. Five of Francis Knock's printed returns to the quarter sessions survive and, like Moran's reports, they include details of many prosecutions between 1853 and 1856. These include cases contrary to the Weights and Measures Act, such as selling bread from a cart without being provided with weights and scales. Superintendent Knock's reports contain more information than his predecessor's, as they also include details on the repair of the division's bridges and of the expenses incurred transporting prisoners to Oxford. One example in 1854 states:

The bridges are all in good repair – except the one at Caversham which is both inconvenient and dangerous owing to its being so narrow.

Francis Knock clearly made an impression on the justices at quarter sessions; at the April 1854 meeting he was described as

Having diligently performed his duties, and has made daily entries in his journal in a neat and intelligent manner. Cases of sheep stealing have occurred in this division, in common with other parts of the county.[150]

Knock received permission to move house from Checkendon to Cane End from the magistrates in 1854, where he stated that he found the performance of his duties facilitated by the change. He continued to impress the magistrates in diligently carrying out his duties, as a newspaper report shows in January 1855, when reporting on duties to the petty sessions:

The Magistrates of the Henley Bench remark that the Superintendent of that Division has shown much skill

---

[150] *Oxford University and City Herald*, 8 April 1854.

*and energy in adopting measures which they anticipate
will subvert a system of plunder which had been carried
on without detection, and in respect of which several
prisoners are now under commitment of trial.*[151]

What these new measures of Knock's were, is not recorded;
however, his returns to the quarter sessions for that quarter
show the following arrests.

1. *Abraham James, stealing money from James Goody
   at Rotherfield Greys.*
2. *George Critchfield, stealing wearing apparel from
   Thomas Evans, Goring. [Critchfield was later
   sentenced to four years' imprisonment.]*
3. *James Payne, breaking into the house of Thomas
   Pigdon, Blacksmith, Cane End and stealing there
   from 2 guns.*
4. *John Hedges and William Higgle, Poaching on land
   occupied by John Noon, Crowmarsh Gifford.*
5. *Anna and Emma Smith, stealing a quantity of turnips
   from [unreadable].*
6. *Richard Watmore and William Kirk, night poaching
   in a wood belonging to H.P. Powys.*
7. *William Ing, stealing a shovel belonging to James
   Bitmead, Labourer, Benson.*
8. *Richard Ambrose, stealing 3 ducks belonging to
   Joseph Paliver, Kidmore End.*
9. *George Allum, riding in a wagon drawn by four horses
   without reins or any person to guide the same.*
10. *James Newman, poaching on land belonging to H.P.
    Powys Esq.*
11. *William Appleton, assaulting William Critchfield,
    Woodman, Whitchurch.*
12. *Mary Jackson and Jane McDonald of no fixed abode,
    stealing a quantity of clothing apparel belonging to
    Jane Thomas, Caversham.*
13. *James Province, stealing hay belonging to Thomas
    Ward, Farmer, South Stoke.*

---

[151] *Oxford Chronicle and Berks & Bucks Gazette*, 6 January 1855.

The quarter sessions stated their concerns that crime had appeared to be increasing over the previous quarter, which was borne out by Knock's report to them early in 1855. He again raised his dissatisfaction with parish constables, too:

> *It would appear that offenders in many cases might have been discovered were not detection prevented by the remissness of parties, including the parish constables, in giving information to the Superintending Constables.*[152]

In his report to the Lent Quarter Sessions in 1855 Superintendent Knock included the following expenses incurred by him of transporting prisoners from Henley to Oxford Gaol:

Thomas Kislingbury and Abraham James	*17s*
James Payne	*17s*
Richard Whatmore and William Kirk	*17s*
William Ing	*17s*
William Appleton	*17s*
James Province	*17s*
Total	£ 5. 2. 0

For the quarter ending March 1855, Knock submitted a claim for expenses. On this claim form he has written, 'Oxfordshire Constabulary – Henley Division'. Was this a mistake by Francis Knock or were there in 1855 moves towards a countywide constabulary in Oxfordshire?

---

[152] *Oxford Chronicle and Berks & Bucks Gazette*, 6 January 1855.

His expenses were listed as follows:

Contingent disbursements necessarily incurred for the use of the division.

Purchase of horse cloth for the use of prisoners conveying them to gaol – 15s.

Lamp candles for cart use in the service – 1s 8d.
Postage of letters on service, excluding parcels – 4s 6d.

Oil and cotton for County lamps – 3s

Total £1.4s 2d.

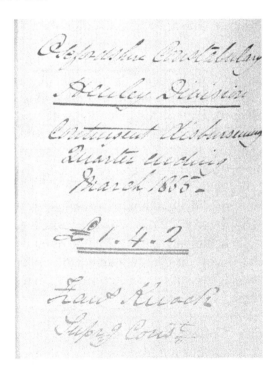

Superintending Constable Knock's quarter
sessions returns for March 1855.[153]

---

[153] Oxfordshire History Centre QS1855/A6/10

County and Borough Police Act 1856

At the Oxfordshire Epiphany Quarter Sessions held on Monday 5 January 1857, it was agreed by the joint committee that the clerk of the peace should be instructed to give formal notice to the superintending constables in Oxfordshire. The notice would state that their services would no longer be required because of the organisation of a county police, as now required by law, unless the chief constable gave them some appointment in connection with the new police force. The justices stated that they were a very deserving body of men and had performed their duties in a satisfactory manner and were deserving all the notice the court could give them.[154]

The superintending constable role in the county officially ended on 8 April 1857, after a period of just six years. Francis Knock had been an experienced police officer before becoming the superintending constable of the Henley division. He brought his knowledge and experience to the role and, for the four years he was in the post, he carried out his duties diligently and with the respect of the magistrates he regularly reported to. His CV and performance as superintending constable clearly impressed the first chief constable of the newly formed Oxfordshire Constabulary, because he was the only one of Oxfordshire's superintending constables to be taken on directly as a police superintendent. Four of his superintending colleagues were recruited as police inspectors.

The Oxfordshire Constabulary recruitment register shows Francis Knock was appointed as a police superintendent on 1 April 1857, aged 40 years; he is described as 5' 9" tall, fair complexion, blue eyes, brown hair with a good figure, and was married with nine children.

---

[154] *Oxford Chronicle*, 10 January 1857.

On 25 May 1857 he was posted to the Bampton East division. In 1861 he was living with his family at Witney Police Station, but the recruitment register later shows that on 23 December 1864 he was dismissed and removed from the force the next day. The reasons for his dismissal are unclear.[155] In 1871 Knock is living in Station Road, Stow on the Wold, as a retired hemp and tent agent. He died at the age of 76 at Foleshill, Warwickshire, in 1894.

In 1856, following a critical report by a select committee of the House of Commons, the County and Borough Police Act was passed. This required the justices to establish a paid police force in each county that did not yet have one. Government inspectors were to visit and inspect all forces annually, to report on their efficiency to the home secretary. The select committee heard evidence from many sources, two of which are of interest here. Maurice Swabey, a Buckinghamshire magistrate who advocated a rural police force in his county, complained that the parish constables in Thame, Oxfordshire, drove vagrants over the border into Buckinghamshire to get rid of them and allay any expense to the parish.

David Smith, the superintending constable in the Chadlington and Banbury South petty sessional division since May 1851, was critical in his evidence of the general inefficiency of the parish constables. He said:

> *Some of them can neither read nor write. Some time ago I had occasion to place a warrant in the hands of a constable; he asked me what it was; I told him to look at it again; he did and said he could not read it. I had no effectual means of discharging him; my only remedy was to report him at the next annual re-election.*[156]

---

[155] *Oxfordshire Constabulary Recruitment Register 1857–1863*. Oxfordshire Black Sheep Publication 2004.
[156] *Oxfordshire Constabulary 1857 Centenary 1957*. Chief Constable.

Oxfordshire Constabulary

At the Oxfordshire Trinity Quarter Sessions on 30 June 1856, the justices appointed a committee to examine the provisions of the County Police Bill with regard to the formation of a county police force. Colonel W. Cartwright, a government inspector general of police, attended a meeting of the committee on 29 December 1856 to advise them. The inspector general proposed the establishment of a force as follows:

1 Chief Constable (who should reside at Oxford) at £300 p.a. plus £100 for travelling and all other expenses.

3 Superintendents at £100 p.a. each with the addition of £40 each to indemnify them for the expense of purchasing and keeping a horse and cart.

5 First Class Inspectors, at £75 p.a. each.

2 Second Class Inspectors, at £65 p.a. each.

6 Sergeants, at £60 p.a. each.

24 First Class Constables, wages of 20/- per week with the prospect of this being increased to 21/- after 2 years' service or for specially good conduct.

24 Second Class Constables, wages of 19/- per week.

24 Third Class Constables, wages 17/- per week.

The equipment for the said Superintendents, Inspectors, Sergeants and Constables consisting of the following articles. In the first year, one great coat with cape and badge, one coat with badge, two pair of trousers, one pair of boots, one pair of shoes and one hat, one stock, a staff, a pair of handcuffs and a lantern. In the second year, one coat with badge, one pair of trousers, one pair of boots, one pair of shoes and one hat.[157]

---

[157] *Oxford Chronicle and Berks and Bucks Gazette*, 10 January 1857.

POLICE.

THE Magistrates of the County of Oxford will proceed to the election of a CHIEF CONSTABLE of the County at an adjourement of the Quarter Sessions, to be held at the County Hall, in Oxford, on Friday, the 27th of February next, at 12 o'clock. Candidates for the office are requested to make application in writing, and to transmit their testimonials to the undersigned on or before the Sixth of February. The Salary will be Three Hundred Pounds, with the addition of One Hundred Pounds per annum for travelling and all other expenses, excepting stationery.

Advertisement for the chief constable of Oxfordshire, *Oxford Chronicle and Berks and Bucks Gazette*, 17 January 1857

On Friday 27 February 1857, the county magistrates met in County Hall, Oxford, to elect a chief constable to organise and superintend the new county police.

The magistrates initially had concerns about any applicant who was a resident in the county. They felt that, given the nature and great responsibility of the role, someone free from local connection and influence would be more likely to succeed. The chairman of the committee, however, stated that all they could do was to judge the testimonials of the candidates about their supposed fitness for the office. They voted to allow candidates from Oxfordshire to apply for the post.

A total of 67 candidates offered themselves, and submitted their testimonials. Of those 67 candidates, three were favoured by the magistrates:

1. *Richard Bridges Bellers, Captain and Adjutant of the Wiltshire Militia.*
2. *Charles Fortunatus Grant, late Captain of the third Regiment of the Bombay Army.*
3. *Mr Charles Mostyn* **OWEN**, *late Assistant High Commissioner of the Cape of Good Hope and organiser of the police.*

Colonel Bowles on the committee nominated a fourth candidate, which was accepted by his colleagues.

4. *William Holloway, Captain of the Oxfordshire Militia.*

The voting went as follows: 37 votes for Mr Owen; 10 votes for Captain Bellers; nine votes for Captain Holloway and one vote for Captain Grant. Mr Owen was duly elected as the first chief constable of Oxfordshire Constabulary. The decision appears to have been made solely on paper references, without interviewing the candidates in person. The Home Office later confirmed their approval of him as chief constable.

Capt. CHARLES MOSTYN OWEN
27 . 2 . 1857 - 2 . 7 1888

Picture: Oxfordshire Constabulary 1857-1957 Centenary book.

Charles Owen was 40 years old and had been born at West Felton, near Shrewsbury, Shropshire, and was married to Fanny. He wasted no time in organising a county police force from scratch. Tenders were submitted for clothing and other accoutrements for the new police force. The clothing was subsequently supplied by Messrs. Dolan and Co., of 87 St Martins Lane, London, and the handcuffs, truncheons, lanterns and cutlasses by Messrs. Parker and Field, of Holborn, London. Charles Owen began his duties as chief constable on 25 March 1857, using offices in the Militia Armoury, Oxford, and he was required to live in Oxford.

Optimism about the new police at Henley was expressed in an editorial in the *Oxford Chronicle and Berks and Bucks Gazette* on 28 February 1857:

Henley on Thames

As the time is fast approaching when this town will be under the guardianship of the new system of police, the inhabitants hope that more attention will be given to its internal management, inasmuch as it is thought that more strength will be given to meet the requirements of the place. The nuisance so long permitted of numbers of persons loitering on the pavements on the corners of the principal streets, polluting the ears of passers-by with the most disgusting and obscene conversation, it is hoped will be prevented, and that the police will not only put a stop to this evil, but that they will use their endeavours to effectually rid the town of the number of beggars with whom it is infected.

One month after the formation of the county constabulary, another article observed that the 'New Police' were already dealing with those nuisances in Henley:

New Police

Several men of this force are now stationed in this town, and we see one important improvement already, the removal of that great nuisance which has become so universally spoken by both strangers and inhabitants, viz; those idle men who blocked up the thoroughfares at the corners of the streets, polluting the ears of the housekeepers and the public by their observations and other abominations. We sincerely hope that this essential body will succeed in their endeavours to rid the public of this evil.[158]

The Oxfordshire Trinity Quarter Sessions received the first report of the chief constable, which began:

To Her Majesty's Justices of the Peace of the County of Oxford, in Quarter Sessions assembled, on Monday 29 June 1857. My Lords and Gentlemen, I have the honour to submit to you the annexed nominal state and disposition of the Constabulary of this County. The conduct of this force (with the exception of a few men whom I have dismissed for misconduct) has been satisfactory, and I hope in the course of another month to have them in a thoroughly complete and efficient state.

The disposition of 83 officers who had been recruited was listed and those who were stationed within the Henley sub-division were named as follows:

Inspector Aquila DUCK. Henley

The unusually named Inspector Duck was born in Willoughby, Sleaford, Lincolnshire. He had previously served for 10 years in the 3rd Dragoons, and joined the force on 1 April 1857 aged 33 years. He was promoted to inspector on 22 June 1857. However, Duck resigned on 22 October 1857 due to drunkenness and irregularities.

Sergeant Daniel HAYWARD. Henley

Sergeant Hayward was born at Easington near Stroud, Gloucestershire, and had previously served with the Royal Marines and Gloucestershire Constabulary. He joined the

---

[158] *Oxford Journal and Berks and Bucks Gazette*, 30 May 1857.

force on 1 April 1857 aged 34 years and was promoted to sergeant on 18 May 1857. He served in the force for 26 years at various stations, retiring in November 1883 with a pension of 19 shillings per week.

Constable Henry SADLER. Caversham

Henry Sadler was born in Oxford and had previous service with the Royal Marines. Aged 30 years, he joined on 1 April 1857. He left on 1 August 1858, with his certificate of service stating that his conduct was generally good.

Constable James CHAMP. Whitchurch

James Champ, aged 25 years, was born in Kennington, Oxford, and had been a labourer before joining on 13 April 1857. He served for a total of 34 years before retiring on a pension of £45 10s per annum.[159]

Constable William HASTINGS. Shiplake

William Hastings had previously worked as a bricklayer before joining the police on 4 May 1857 aged 22 years. He was born in Wallingford and was discharged on 19 December 1859 and fined 2 shillings and sixpence for neglecting to make entries in his diary for 11 days.

Constable David PITTS. Rotherfield Grays

David Pitts was born at Souldern, Brackley, Northamptonshire. He had previously worked on the Great Western Railway and joined the police on 13 April 1857 aged 25 years. He served for 24 years and resigned in January 1881 on a pension of £32 18s 8d per annum.

Constable George HARRIS. Crowmarsh

George Harris was born at Kingham, Oxfordshire, and had previous service with the Scots Fusilier Guards for nine years. Aged 29 years, he joined the police on 27 April 1857.

---

[159] The photograph of Constable Champ is held in the TVP Museum Sulhampstead

On 30 December 1867 he was ordered to resign and removed from the force.

Constable Charles GOULD. Goring

Charles Gould was born in Curbridge, Witney, Oxfordshire. Before joining the police aged 22 years, he worked as a labourer in Cambridge. He joined on 1 May 1857. He was dismissed from the force on 18 March 1858 after drinking and dancing in a public house when on duty.

Police Constable 29, James Champ

Constable George BOWERS. Henley

George Bowers was a labourer who was born at St Aldates, Oxford. Aged 32 years, he joined on 28 May 1857. He had

116

13 years' previous service with the 23rd Regiment (Royal Welch Fusiliers). He served for just six months before resigning on 10 November 1857.

Constable Edward WILLIAMS. Henley

Edward Williams had three years' previous service with the Metropolitan Police before joining Oxfordshire Constabulary on 30 April 1857. He was born at Little Missenden, Bucks. On 13 August 1866, while a sergeant, he drank on duty at Henley and was reduced to first class constable and required to resign. He was discharged on 20 August 1866.

These short biographies come from the *Oxfordshire Constabulary Recruitment Registers 1857–1863*, published by Black Sheep Publications in 2004. More details of these and other officers who were later posted to Henley and other stations, and who made up the first recruits of the whole of the Oxfordshire Constabulary, can be seen in that publication.

In April 1857, Henley formed part of 'A' Division, part of Force Headquarters, Bullingdon and Watlington. Acting superintendent Thomas Moulden was in charge of the division and was based at Watlington.

The chief constable reported on the station house at Henley, which was owned by the Corporation, who required a rent of £18 per annum. He proposed to charge the constables who lodged there from £11 to £14 a year. He further stated that the house was large, and a room may be reserved for the use of the county as a charge room. He asked to be allowed to rent it on the terms specified above.[160]

One inspector, a sergeant and two constables would appear to us now to be insufficient to police the town; however, this number was supplemented by the Corporation's own

---

[160] *Oxford Journal*, 4 July 1857.

parochial constables, one of them being Henry Stephens, and the town in the 1850s would have had a population of approximately 3,700.[161]

Henley police station

In May 1868 a notice was issued in local newspapers for persons willing to convert two houses and ground bought by the county on West Hill, Henley, into a police station.

Plans and specifications could be inspected at the offices of the architect, William Wilkinson, 5 Beaumont Street, Oxford, and tenders were to be submitted to the clerk to the peace by 28 May 1868. The plans for the police station had been approved by the secretary of state and in July 1868 John Willis, of Nettlebed, won the tender for the sum of £1,093.

In January 1869 the conversion was complete and ready for occupation. The premises were enlarged and access improved in 1892, and again in July 1898. It was partly rebuilt in 1913 by Bosher & Sons of Cholsey, Berks, for £1,750.

Henley-on-Thames police station 1869–2000s

Banbury was the only Oxfordshire town not to amalgamate its police force with the county force in 1857; it waited a further 68 years, until 1925, when two sergeants and 11 constables from Banbury Borough Police transferred to Oxfordshire Constabulary.[162]

Oxfordshire Constabulary existed for 116 years, until it was compulsorily amalgamated with Berkshire Constabulary, Buckinghamshire Constabulary, Oxford City Police and Reading Borough Police on 1 April 1968 to form the Thames Valley Constabulary,[163] which became Thames Valley Police in 1974.

Thames Valley Constabulary helmet plate (author's collection)

---

[162] *Banbury Constables 1775–1925*. Oxfordshire Black Sheep Publication 2005.
[163] Report of Inquiry. HMSO Police Act 1964.

Chapter Seven

Henley constables and dates they are known to have served up to 1857

John GRAVETT	1542
Richard COLLINS	1542
Augustine SPRINGALL	1592–1622
Thomas HARRIS	1704
William FOSTER	1704
George HAMPSHIRE	1715
Sampson TOOVEY	1715
Henry GREEN	1716
John LOVEGROVE	1716
John STEVENS	1717
Thomas MASON	1717
John HAVERGILL	1718
William DEANE	1718
John BUTLER	1719
William WOODHOUSE	1719
Thomas PATEY	1720
James LAMDON	1720
George JEMMAT	1722
John SMITH	1722
William BROOKS	1723
Abraham DARBY	1723
Stephen FLETCHER	1724
William NEWBERRY	1724
John TOOVEY	1725
Joseph DEANE	1725
Benjamin WOOLDBRIDGE	1726
Thomas HAVERGILL	1726
John EELES	1727

Thomas CASBIRD	1727
William PRAT	1728
Thomas JOHNSON	1728
Thomas TAYLOR Jun.	1729
Henry ROGERS	1729
John CORDEROY	1730
Robert STOPES	1730
Samuel SILLS	1731
John HOLLYER	1731
Samuel HUCKS	1732
Moses HIGGS	1732
William SHARP	1733
Peter STOPES	1733
William BENWELL	1734
Robert KITSON	1734
Richard DARBY	1735
Thomas SPINDLER	1735
Robert LOVEDAY	1786
John WHITE	1786
John ARUNDELL	1800
Richard TAYLOR	1800
William HORSLEY	1825
Thomas LIVINGSTONE	1827/28
? WHITE	1829
Richard POTTER‡	1831–1834
James LOFTING	1833
Thomas SMITH	1834
John MOSS	1834
Henry STEPHENS	1834–1862
John WICHELO	1836–1840?
Samuel CARTER	1841–1845
Joseph BALLARD	1848-1853
Matthew MORAN*	1851–1853
Thomas BOLTON	1854–1857
Francis KNOCK*	1853–1857

‡ First salaried constable and serving more than the one year, unlike unpaid parish constables.
* Superintending constable of the Henley petty sessional division.

Bibliography

ALASIA, V.: *Henley Union Workhouse*. Brewin Books (2016).

BEATTY, J.M.: *The First English Detectives*. Oxford University Press (2012).

BRITISH NEWSPAPER LIBRARY: Newspaper records researched through FindmyPast.com.

BURNS, J.S.: *A History of Henley*. Longman & Co. (1861).

COTTINGHAM, A.: *The Hostelries of Henley*. Parchment, Oxford (2000).

CRITCHLEY. T.A.: *A History of Police in England and Wales*. Constable & Co (1979).

FOSTER, D.: *The Rural Constabulary Act 1839*. Bedford Square Press (1982).

GIBSON, R.: *Historic Town Centre Survey. Henley on Thames 1990–1993*. Henley Archaeological & Historical Group. Digital version processed by David Feary 2021.

HART, Jenifer: 'Reform of the Borough Police, 1835–1856'. *The English Historical Review Advertiser* (January 1936).

HENLEY TOWN COUNCIL. Fairmile Cemetery Records.

KARAU, P.: *The Henley-on-Thames Branch*. Wild Swan Publications (1982).

OXFORDSHIRE CONSTABULARY: *Centenary Booklet 1857–1957*. Chief Constable: Testro Bros.

OXFORDSHIRE HISTORY CENTRE: Diverse Oxfordshire Quarter Sessions & Henley Borough Records.

PIGOT'S Directory 1842/44.

PRINGLE, P.: *Hue and Cry. The Birth of the British Police*. London Museum Press Ltd (1955).

RAWLINGS, P.: *Policing: A Short History*. Willan Publishing (2002).

RICHMOND, C.: *Oxfordshire Constabulary Recruitment Register 1857–1863*. Oxfordshire Black Sheep Publications (2004).

—*Henley on Thames Poor Relief, Vol. 2: 1822–1835*. (2008) and

—*Banished! Sentences of Transportation from Oxfordshire Courts 1787–1867*. (2007).

RIPLEY, H.: *Police Forces of Great Britain and Ireland – Their Amalgamations and their Buttons*. R. Hazell & Co. (1983).

ROTHWELL, M.: *Policing the West Country*. CreateSpace Independent Publishing Platform (2017).

SCOLLAN, Maureen: *Sworn to Serve. Police in Essex*. Phillimore & Co. Ltd (1993).

SLEIGH, Captain A.W.: *A General Police and Constabulary List and Analysis of Criminal and Police Statistics for the Quarter Ending September 1844*. Parker, Furnival and Parker. Reproduced by the Police History Society. Original held in the Lancashire Record Office.

STALLION, M. & WALL, D.: *The British Police. Forces and Chief Officers 1829–2012*. 2nd edition. MPG Books Group (2011).

STATE LIBRARY of QUEENSLAND: British Convict Transportation Register, available online.

St MARY'S CHURCH, Henley on Thames. Baptism, Marriage and Burial Records. CD Vol 4. OFHS 1994 to 2005.

TAYLOR, M.B. & WILKINSON, V.L.: *Badges of Office. An Illustrated Guide to the Helmets and Badges of the British Police 1829 to 1989*. R. Hazell & Co. (Republished 1995 by the Police Insignia Collectors Association of GB).

TOMALIN, G.H.J.: *The Book of Henley on Thames*. Barracuda Books Ltd (1975).

TOWNLEY, Dr S.: *A History of the County of Oxford. Volume XVI Henley on Thames and Environs*. Boydell & Brewer (2011).

Acknowledgements

I wish to acknowledge the help I received in researching the history of Henley-on-Thames' police. The date of formation of a salaried constabulary was uncertain until the staff at the Oxford History Centre produced the 1830 document of the Corporation of Henley-on-Thames committee looking to establish a more efficient police in the town. From this document the transformation from parish to salaried constables began, although those constables continued in their other occupations too, because the policing pay was not sufficient to make it a full-time occupation. My thanks to the staff of the Oxfordshire History Centre, who were able to provide numerous documents on-line despite lockdown during the Covid pandemic.

Dr Simon Townley, editor of *A History of the County of Oxford. Volume XVI, Henley on Thames and Environs*, who kindly clarified the details of the several Bridge Acts, which gave the mayor the authority to appoint parish and then salaried constables in the town.

To Peter Neyroud CBE QPM CCMI ex Chief Constable of Thames Valley Police, who kindly agreed to write the foreword to this publication.

The author would also like to extend his thanks to the trustees of the Lamborn Greening Trust, whose valuable contribution enabled publication of this book.

'The Greening Lamborn Trust's objective is to promote public interest in the history, architecture, old photographs and heritage of Oxford and its neighbourhood by supporting publications and other media that creates access to them.'

The Author

Andrew King was born in Henley-on-Thames and attended Gillotts School. He joined the Thames Valley Constabulary in 1971, and attended the No.5 Regional Training Centre, Eynsham Hall, North Leigh, Witney, Oxon. He served in uniform for five years, before completing the Metropolitan Police Detective Training Course at Peel House, Hendon, in 1977. Andrew then worked on CID, Special Branch and the Fraud Squad, where he undertook various investigations that involved overseas travel to the Russian Federation, British Virgin Islands and the USA. Following his retirement from the Thames Valley Police after 32 years, Andrew worked as a fraud investigator for a private accountancy firm, and undertook overseas fraud enquiries in South Africa, Senegal, Mauritania and Malawi, on behalf of the Department for International Development and Oxfam. He is a member of the Police History Society and the Oxfordshire Family History Society.

Milton Keynes UK
Ingram Content Group UK Ltd.
UKHW030736070824
446656UK00002B/40

9 781803 814636